Second Edition

Creating Physical & Emotional Security in Schools

KENNETH C. WILLIAMS

A Joint Publication

Solution Tree

naesp™

Essentials for Principals is a registered trademark of the National Association of Elementary School Principals.

555 North Morton Street
Bloomington, IN 47404
800.733.6786 (toll free) / 812.336.7700
FAX: 812.336.7790

email: info@solution-tree.com
solution-tree.com

Printed in the United States of America

16 15 14 13 12   1 2 3 4 5

Library of Congress Cataloging-in-Publication Data

Williams, Kenneth C.

   Essentials for principals : creating physical and emotional security in schools / Kenneth C. Williams. -- 2nd ed.

      p. cm.

   Includes bibliographical references and index.

   ISBN 978-1-935542-78-0 (perfect bound : alk. paper) -- ISBN 978-1-935542-79-7 (library bound : alk. paper) 1. Schools--Security measures--United States--Handbooks, manuals, etc. 2. Schools--United States--Safety measures--Handbooks, manuals, etc. 3. School environment--United States--Handbooks, manuals, etc.. 4. School crisis management--United States--Handbooks, manuals, etc. 5. Classroom management--United States--Handbooks, manuals, etc. 6. Behavior modification--United States--Handbooks, manuals, etc. 7. School discipline--United States--Handbooks, manuals, etc. 8. Elementary school principals--United States--Handbooks, manuals, etc. I. Title.

   LB2866.W55 2012

   370.71'1--dc23

                    2012015134

Solution Tree

Jeffrey C. Jones, CEO
Edmund M. Ackerman, President

Solution Tree Press

President: Douglas M. Rife
Publisher: Robert D. Clouse
Vice President of Production: Gretchen Knapp
Managing Production Editor: Caroline Wise
Senior Production Editor: Suzanne Kraszewski
Proofreader: Ashante Thomas
Text Designer: Jenn Taylor
Cover Designer: Rian Anderson

To my mother and father, who—every day of my life—made me believe I could accomplish anything. To my wife, Nicole, and our children, Adam and Mia, for giving of themselves so that I can live my passion. I love you all so much.

ACKNOWLEDGMENTS

I am grateful to Douglas Rife for approaching me about writing this volume in the *Essentials for Principals* series. I am honored to be among the authors involved in this project, and I thank Douglas for sharing his personal wisdom and experience with me. I also thank Solution Tree's entire publishing team for their assistance, suggestions, and support—especially Claudia Wheatley, Gretchen Knapp, and Sue Kraszewski. Their patience with me allowed for this breakthrough in my career of which I am proud.

To the dedicated school principals and assistant principals with whom I've worked—you understand what it is to be both leaders and learners. I've learned from many of you what it means to "set the table" for learning—how having effective systems to support physical and emotional security in schools is critical for a powerful culture of learning. You do the hard work of school improvement every day, always striving for continuous improvement in the service of ensuring high levels of learning for all students. Thank you for your transparency and for your willingness to talk about what did and did not work.

I would also like to thank my professional mentors, Rick DuFour, Becky DuFour, Bob Eaker, and Jeff Jones, who gave me the wonderful opportunity to train, speak, inspire, consult, and write. They saw more potential in me than I saw in myself. I thank them for this gift of opportunity. I also thank Anthony Muhammad and Mike Mattos, two great colleagues and friends, who put in overtime as my mentors as well. I appreciate your honesty, candor, and abundant generosity.

To Lindsay Carleton, my personal writing "guide on the side"—thank you for taking my written word and giving it a flow while maintaining my voice. Thank you to Shannon Ritz, Kendra Clark, and the entire professional development team at Solution Tree for providing the support that allows me to work with so many practitioners across North America. And to my consultant colleagues in the Solution Tree family, the amount of resources, support, and encouragement you provide is staggering. Thank you for such selfless giving.

I would also like to thank the practitioners in the field—the administrators and school leaders who work in the trenches every day. Many started out as clients, some have become colleagues, and in several cases, friends. I hold you in high regard for making every day another opportunity to implement best practices for effective student learning. I wish I could name all those whose paths I've crossed. Some who provided specific insights and examples for this book include Michael Bayewitz, principal at Broad Acres Elementary in Silver Spring, Maryland; Catherine Smith, principal at Evoline C. West Elementary in Fairburn, Georgia; Taylor Harper, administrator at Washoe

Inspire Academy in Reno, Nevada; and Cory Radisch, principal of Maple Place Middle School in Oceanport, New Jersey.

Finally, I must acknowledge my phenomenal family. They are my foundation. It starts with my parents, Carl and Suzanne Williams—my first teachers and mentors. While sometimes lacking in financial resources, you found ways to provide me with a wealth of opportunities. You have and still make me feel and believe that I can accomplish anything. My beautiful and supportive wife, Nicole, along with our wonderful kids, Adam and Mia, have been my biggest fans. Thank you for allowing me the space to live, learn, and grow in this work. Thank you for helping me believe I can do anything, for dealing with me, and for keeping me grounded as well. I love all of you dearly.

Solution Tree Press would like to thank the following reviewers:

Mike Anderson
Professional Development Specialist
Durham, New Hampshire

Tracy Barber
Principal
Okolona Elementary
Louisville, Kentucky

Kevin R. Booker
Associate Dean of Student Life
Morehouse College
Atlanta, Georgia

Michael J. Corso
Chief Academic Officer
Quaglia Institute for Student Aspirations
Waltham, Massachusetts

Scott Dodson
Principal
Woodland Park Elementary School
Norfolk, Nebraska

Kelsey Augst Felton
School Counselor
Hilburn Drive Academy
Raleigh, North Carolina

Gregory Ford
Principal
Hilburn Drive Academy
Raleigh, North Carolina

Phil Hunsberger
Senior Partner, Educational Equity Consultants
Past Director, International Network of
    Principals' Centers
St. Louis, Missouri

Deborah Pattee
Assistant Professor, Department of Education
    Studies
University of Wisconsin-Eau Claire
Eau Claire, Wisconsin

Marti Phillips
Principal
Hull-Jackson Montessori Magnet School
Nashville, Tennessee

Jeannie Richmond-Lynch
Principal
B. C. Haynie Elementary School
Morrow, Georgia

Kim Wellons
Former Principal
Princeton Elementary School
Princeton, North Carolina

Todd Wilmore
Associate Graduate Faculty, Department of
    Education
Central Michigan University
Dalton, Georgia

TABLE OF CONTENTS

ABOUT THE AUTHOR

 **Kenneth C. Williams** is a former teacher, assistant principal, and principal. He shares his experience and expertise as a recognized trainer, speaker, coach, and consultant in education and leadership. Ken is the chief visionary officer of Unfold the Soul, LLC, a company dedicated to inspiring individuals and teams to perform at the highest level. Ken is a former principal of The Learning Academy at E. J. Swint Elementary in Jonesboro, Georgia, and Damascus Elementary in Damascus, Maryland. His firsthand experience with transforming challenged schools translates into action-oriented presentations that inspire hope, create a clear vision, and offer practical strategies to those overwhelmed by challenges.

His leadership was crucial to creating a successful professional learning community (PLC) at Damascus. The results of his efforts can be seen across all grade levels. Over a two-year period, the school's state standardized test scores revealed a significant increase in the percentage of students performing at proficient and advanced levels. The process of building a PLC at E. J. Swint continues thanks to Ken's work in laying the solid foundation in this underserved community.

He is a contributor to the anthology *The Collaborative Administrator: Working Together as a Professional Learning Community*, he has authored book reviews for the *Journal of Staff Development*, and he published an article in Learning Forward's *The Learning Principal*.

Ken earned a bachelor of arts from Morehouse College, a master of science from the University of Bridgeport, and an administration and supervision certificate from Bowie State University.

To learn more about Ken's work, visit www.unfoldthesoul.com.

To book Ken for professional development, contact pd@solution-tree.com.

INTRODUCTION

*What is worth fighting for is not to let
our schools be negative by default, but to
make them positive by design.*

—MICHAEL FULLAN AND CLIF ST. GERMAIN

Many years ago, when my wife and I purchased our first home, we were excited, overjoyed, and very broke. We quickly discovered that we would have to make many improvements to the house ourselves, including replacing old carpet with wood flooring. As I headed to the local home-improvement store, I envisioned what materials I would need: wood flooring (of course), a hammer, nails, varnish, and glue. Many do-it-yourselfers would scoff at my ignorance, but I was truly surprised to find that glue was not a part of the floor-laying process. I discovered that laying wood flooring involves tongue-and-groove technology: a tongue along the edge of one board fits into a groove along the edge of the other board. When I was done laying my new wood floor, I was amazed at how solid and seamless it was.

In the years since I installed that floor, many wonderful things have happened in my house—we had children and watched them grow and experience life, we learned together, we celebrated. The floor I installed provided a solid foundation for our everyday lives. The work of laying a solid foundation in one's home is not unlike the work a principal does to create a solid foundation within his or her school.

Much of the focus in schools is on what happens between teachers and students in the classroom—and understandably so. What is often taken for granted is the foundation upon which learning takes place. If this foundation is firm, then learning can happen. If it's not, students and staff members suffer. Principals create this foundation for learning when they ensure physical and emotional safety in their schools in a purposeful and intentional way. These two elements fit together tongue-and-groove to provide a firm foundation. In the past, principals addressed issues of physical and emotional security by checking boxes off a list, but school leaders now face very different times in which creating a safe school environment is a top priority. If principals neglect to do so, the results can be devastating.

Common sense tells us that when students feel unsafe or unwelcomed, they do not want to be in school and they cannot learn to the best of their abilities because the environment prevents success. At the heart of a physically and emotionally safe school is a caring learning community in which students feel safe, welcomed, cared for, and supported. In such an environment, students are in a much better position to learn and grow, and they have a firm foundation for school success.

What Is a Caring Learning Community?

A caring learning community is easier felt than described; it can feel like magic, though it is actually the result of focused, sustained work. A caring learning community insists on respect for all members. It puts a priority on recognizing and celebrating each individual's abilities and on fostering meaningful student-to-adult and student-to-student relationships. A caring learning community seeks to embed this level of respect, recognition, and celebration as a routine part of the overall school culture. A caring learning community has high expectations for student behavior. It emphasizes and reinforces positive behavior, and school leaders work with staff to develop a schoolwide discipline plan to spell out expectations and ensure physical and emotional safety for all students. Principals play an important role in shaping and maintaining such an environment; they can be thought of as a lighthouse, consistently providing direction and safe harbor.

School is where many students spend most of their waking hours, and it is critically important that they feel a deep sense of connection, support, and safety there. In a caring learning community, every single student feels welcomed and supported every day. Each student should know that there is an adult who is happy to see that he or she arrives at school each day. But a caring learning community isn't simply characterized by what leaders and staff do from a social and emotional standpoint. The atmosphere of acceptance, belonging, and support within a caring learning community makes the ground fertile for learning. Mardale Dunsworth and Dawn Billings (2009) contend that, because of their unique position in the school and district structures, school leaders must set and maintain high expectations for themselves, students, teachers, and all others within the school community. According to Dunsworth and Billings (2009), effective school leaders do the following:

- Create a culture of high expectations for student and adult success and support those beliefs schoolwide

- Foster a positive school environment in which students and staff members feel valued, students are challenged to grow academically, and staff members are challenged to grow professionally

- Create a physical environment that is safe, welcoming, and conducive to learning

- Implement an effective system of discipline and behavior management that supports teaching and learning schoolwide

These elements combine to create the foundation of a caring learning community. Although many responsibilities for creating and maintaining such a community should be shared among staff members, certain responsibilities should not be delegated. Because of their unique position in the school and district, principals must take the lead, setting and maintaining high expectations for themselves, students, teachers, and all others within the school community. Such leadership ensures that the following conditions are established (Dunsworth & Billings, 2009):

- There is an atmosphere of academic press in which learning is prioritized as the most important mission of the school.

- Students feel valued by school administrators and challenged to grow academically.

- Schoolwide positive behavior supports a strong climate for teaching and learning.

- Staff members feel simultaneously valued by school administrators and challenged to grow professionally.

- There is an atmosphere of mutual respect that exists at all levels of the organization and between all stakeholders.

Reculturing Your School

School culture is often slow to change. School leaders naturally place time and energy into the areas they deem to be the most important. As Anne Conzemius and Terry Morganti-Fisher (2012) note, what is given time, energy, and attention will grow. The underlying challenge for educators is identifying the right thing to focus on amidst an endless stream of worthy options. For too many, the trap of business creates a barrier to thoughtful focus resulting in a continuous cycle of work for the sake of getting things done. Leaders must remember that no improvements can fully flourish within a school that does not ensure both physical and emotional security for students. Principals must make sure this critical foundation is set before steering students toward their great potential.

A successful journey does not begin with the first step but rather with a turn to face in the right direction. Likewise, transforming the culture of your school does not start with implementing a sequence of tasks but with creating clarity on the organization's direction: its fundamental purpose (Buffum, Mattos, & Weber, 2012). Before principals take the first steps to creating a caring learning community, they should take a moment to think about every person in the school building. Are they facing the same direction? Teachers will have different levels of comfort, agreement, and understanding when it comes to any initiative. Some will be on board more than others. Some will need additional support. The key to getting everyone to look in the same direction—whether it's to focus on emotional security, physical security, or high expectations for student learning—is by first looking at your school's core values and beliefs. Daniel Goleman (2002) contends that a visionary leader helps people move toward a shared hope or dream, but also allows them to innovate, experiment, and take calculated risks. This has an immensely positive impact on a school's emotional climate.

Warren Bennis (1997), in his work studying what makes both great groups and great leaders, reminds us that "all great teams—and all great organizations—are built around a shared dream or motivating purpose." Every single person on staff should have an opportunity to contribute to the clear picture of the school they want to become and help to build a plan of tangible and observable next steps to bring the vision to reality.

Chapter Overviews

Creating Physical & Emotional Security in Schools provides strategies principals can use in both small- and big-picture ways to facilitate a secure environment and develop strategies to support teachers through observation, communication, and collaboration.

Chapter 1 defines a caring learning community and puts principals on the right track to developing one, detailing the ways in which educators can nurture supportive relationships with their students, develop student initiative and resilience, establish high expectations, encourage celebration, promote parent involvement, and create a positive and welcoming school building.

Chapter 2 focuses on helping students deal with conflict and anger by examining the roots of these feelings and actions, how to integrate conflict-management strategies into the school building, and how to develop schoolwide conflict-management strategies for problem solving and conflict resolution.

Chapter 3 looks at how to develop an effective schoolwide policy for behavior and discipline that focuses on teaching behavioral expectations and using reinforcement and positive rewards, as well as how the main office can address challenging behavior and how to use data for plan improvement.

Chapter 4 addresses how educators can prevent bullying, including cyberbullying, as well as how to enlist the help of parents and school counselors.

Chapter 5 addresses issues of safety and security, including tips for creating a physically safe environment and planning for a crisis.

Developing a Caring Learning Community

*For many students, particularly those
at risk of school failure, the caring
relationship often must precede their
engagement with subject matter.*

—JONATHA W. VARE AND KATHRYN S. MILLER

Have you ever walked into a school that feels qualitatively different? A school that is more than just "good"? In these schools, interactions between students, teachers, and other staff members are warm and positive. These buildings seem to hum with productive activity, and evidence of the high value placed on student work and learning is everywhere. In these schools, a critical connection has been made between students' academic needs and their need to feel emotionally and physically safe, accepted, and valued. These schools are caring learning communities.

A caring learning community is especially important for today's students, some of whom might not have adult role models outside of school to model a caring ethic. However, it is not uncommon in the current educational environment for school leaders to abandon any concern for the culture of the school. The most important thing has been the intense focus on standards and accountability. Donna Marriott (2001) notes that:

> High academic standards, rigorous assessment of student achievement, and teacher preparedness have been cast as the dominant components in current educational reform agendas. (p. 75)

A caring learning community is critical, however, because as Jonatha W. Vare and Kathryn S. Miller (2000) note, a caring relationship is necessary for students to engage in academic learning. Indeed, a culture of caring is the most direct road to sustained academic improvement. This belief is echoed by others. Marriot (2001) goes on to say that high standards, rigorous assessment, and teacher preparedness "have little chance for long-term success unless they are embedded within a positive and productive school culture" (p. 75). Anthony Muhammad, former principal of Glenn Levey Middle School in Southfield, Michigan—a National School of Excellence—explained that until his school "created a safe, orderly campus that addressed students' social and emotional needs, it could not address their academic needs" (Buffum, Mattos, & Weber, 2008, p. 122). As Muhammad noted, while an environment of emotional and physical security is necessary for student success, school leaders should not focus solely on social and emotional needs, and when that's done, then address academic concerns. Many schools have adopted this fragmented approach as an excuse not to address the role of relevant and engaging instruction as a part of a caring learning community.

As a leader, I never felt this connection between academic achievement and a caring community as strongly as when I led a school that had high levels of poverty, low achievement rates, and little sense of community. Improved student achievement was our identified priority, but as I walked down the halls each day, I could see that the school's social and emotional challenges severely hindered our goal of improving student achievement. It made sense that students would be more likely to achieve if every one of them felt upon entering the building that they were emotionally and physically secure—that someone there was glad to see them, cared that they were there, and expected them to learn. Together, with my staff and other stakeholders, we embarked on the journey of creating such a school culture.

Developing Student Initiative

As many educators know, engaging students can sometimes be a struggle. It may seem as though some students simply don't care about what it is they are being asked to learn, but, more often, these students do not feel capable of success. Further, they are afraid of failure and of "looking stupid" in front of peers or teachers. In a caring learning community, students feel capable of taking on challenges. They feel supported and valued as team members, and they are not intimidated by failure. Some students do develop this kind of attitude naturally but many do not. School leaders can help these students develop initiative by fostering a community that enables students to feel interested, supported, and capable—emotionally safe. Specifically, principals can establish and communicate high academic and behavioral expectations, help foster resilience, and create an atmosphere in which students are encouraged to take responsible risks.

Establishing High Academic Expectations

Research suggests that when teachers have high expectations for themselves and their students, it has a direct impact on students' academic achievement (Ross, 1995), and these high expectations are closely tied to caring. Wilson and Corbett (2001, as cited in Muhammad, 2009) describe a study done at five of Philadelphia's lowest-performing middle schools. In the study, researchers spoke with students to discover the types of teachers they felt they needed and wanted. They found that students wanted teachers who were "strict but fair, nice and respectful, and who took the time to explain their lessons to them clearly and effectively. They wanted teachers who believed in them and taught them in the ways that they learned best" (pp. 22–23).

High expectations should not, however, be used to create an environment of judgment. Rather, the goal should be establishing trust. In his study of 120 world-class concert pianists, sculptors, swimmers, tennis players, mathematicians, and research neurologists, Benjamin Bloom found that, for most of them, their first teachers were extremely warm and accepting. They did not set low standards; they created an atmosphere of trust, not judgment. It was, "I'm going to teach you," not, "I'm going to judge your talent" (Dweck, 2007).

Neal Cross (2008) suggests that teachers should be explicit about the relationship between effort and achievement. This means that teachers relay to students that people are not just "born smart" but that they are able to "get smart" with effort. Cross explains:

> Low-achieving students often attribute school failure to factors beyond their control—a lack of innate intelligence, unfairly difficult assignments, or bad luck. It's vital that teachers "retrain" them, helping them attribute failure and difficulty to things they can control: studying hard enough and applying the correct learning strategy. Teachers can help students understand that in most classes, students achieve good scores by listening, trying, trying again, reading, asking questions, paying attention, asking for help, being serious, and reading critically. (p. 27)

It is dangerous for educators to set low expectations for students. Clearly this is wrong when it is the result of discrimination that links perceived student ability to such factors as race, gender, socioeconomic standards, and the like. However, sometimes low expectations are the result of positive intentions. Educators who make this mistake are, as a principal once told me, confusing sympathy and empathy. *Sympathy* allows us to identify with the issues, circumstances, and factors students bring to the learning environment that may interfere with their learning: we feel deeply for students, so we lower our expectations. *Empathy* also allows us to feel deeply for students' struggles; however, we are able to contextualize them. We do not lower expectations; rather, a student's background frames the context for the school's response.

In a caring learning community, school leaders and teachers acknowledge issues that their students have—personal, behavioral, academic, and so forth—and work with students to maintain high expectations despite challenges. This empathetic stance empowers leaders and teachers to help students overcome challenges.

Principals play a vital role in keeping expectations high for all learners. They must incorporate academic support and feedback into their caring learning community. Leaders cannot simply set or expect high expectations for students and wash their hands of the matter of achievement. Students need assistance along the way; they need to actually see, in both small and large ways, that success is a real, achievable thing.

Establishing High Expectations for Behavior

High expectations should extend to student behavior as well. It is important that students are held to high standards of citizenship, including kindness to and respect for peers and adults. It must also be made clear to students that teachers and other adults in the school hold themselves to the same high standards (Wagner, 1999). These high standards of citizenship begin in the classroom, where teachers can help students develop self-discipline and take responsibility for their own behavior. The Learning First Alliance (2001) suggests providing students with opportunities for:

> Voice and choice . . . [which] strengthens students' bonds and commitment to the school community. By helping to define the school's goals and plan its activities, students see the school as "theirs" and prepare for the demanding role of productive citizenship in our democracy. (p. 10)

While shifting to a culture of high expectations isn't a task solely for the school principal, this shift typically starts with the school principal. Principals must communicate high expectations and provide support and resources for these expectations. The primary way of establishing high expectations for behavior is through a schoolwide behavior-management plan that staff work collaboratively to create that emphasizes and supports positive behaviors and addresses undesirable behaviors with appropriate consequences. (This is explored in more detail in chapter 3.)

Developing Student Resilience

Another way leaders can help students develop initiative is by helping them develop resilience. *Resilience* is the ability to bounce back from setbacks and failures and to pursue goals even in the face of overwhelming odds. The American Psychological Association (1996) has identified factors, many of which can be fostered in a school setting, that promote resilience. These include:

- Positive role models

- Exposure to a greater number of positive rather than negative behaviors

- Development of self-esteem and self-efficacy

- Supportive relationships, including those with teachers and friends

- A sense of hope about the future

- Belief in oneself

- Strong social skills

- Good peer relationships

- A close, trusting bond with a nurturing adult outside the family

- The sense that one is in control of one's life and can cope with whatever happens

Ask a resilient adult what he or she considered to be of most importance in assisting him or her to overcome adversity in childhood, and invariably the first response will be "someone who believed in me and stood by me." Julius Segal (1988), who devoted much of his life as a psychologist to exploring what helps at-risk youngsters to survive and thrive, noted:

> Researchers have distilled a number of factors that enable children of misfortune to beat the heavy odds against them. One factor turns out to be the presence of a charismatic adult—a person with whom they can identify and

from whom they gather strength. And in a surprising number of cases, that person turns out to be a teacher. (p. 3)

Some students come by resilience naturally, but others do not, and if leaders can help to instill qualities of resilience in students, those students are more likely to feel supported and capable. A caring learning community includes many of the factors that develop resilience and adults that care for each and every student in the school.

Developing Close Relationships With Adults

Teachers and administrators cannot simply *tell* students that they care; they must *show* students how they care and how to care by cultivating caring relationships with them. Cohen (2001) suggests that the following factors be a part of a supportive school environment. These elements are part of a caring learning community in which students feel emotionally and physically secure:

- Opportunities for students to interact with adults outside of the classroom, such as at school concerts, sporting events, and fundraisers

- Opportunities for students to share concerns and problems with adults who respond in a helpful way

- Access to adults who are willing to provide one-on-one guidance and mentoring on academic issues

- Access to adults who maintain consistent and proactive contact with the home

- Mutual trust and respect between school and home and between adults and students in the school

Sometimes strategies designed to help promote a caring learning community (such as teacher advisories or tutoring programs) are contradicted by messages in the school's "hidden curriculum" (Educational Research Service, 1997), which is made up of the subtle and often unintended messages of everyday interactions or the environment. Leaders should carefully consider the extent to which elements of the hidden curriculum—including the attitudes and actions of school staff and the physical environment of the school—communicate caring and respect for all school community members. Leaders and school staff should avoid behaviors like sarcasm and favoritism that can undermine students' dignity or self-esteem (Lickona, 1991). All staff members must realize that what they don't do or do subconsciously can have a huge impact on students.

Student-adult connections are a very powerful way to create a caring learning community that enables high achievement and allows students to feel emotionally and physically safe; however, it isn't an easy task. With the rush of daily events and the many demands and competing priorities in schools, it's easy for a well-intentioned principal and staff to allow these connections to slip through the cracks. Principals must remember that connections are only established in part by the attitudes of the adults in the school; structures are also necessary to facilitate and develop adult-student relationships.

In one school in which I worked, there was a distinct pattern of failure, which was exacerbated by the fact that students came from very challenging backgrounds and brought some of the remnants of their adversity to school every day. From the outside looking in, our school's situation seemed overwhelming. In attempting to build connections with students, we did what Mike Mattos and Laurie Robinson (personal communication, June 2010) call "giving data a face." As a principal, I worked to forge one-on-one relationships between adults and between adults and students, hoping to give our data a face. Eventually, instead of focusing on the cavalcade of problems and issues facing us as a school, staff members focused on the individual students with whom they had built relationships. This individual responsibility would come in a myriad of forms. Sometimes it was a student getting extra help, sometimes it was mentoring, and sometimes it was via a club or an activity. The more adults connected with students, the more invested the adults became in those students. The reverse was true as well; the more students saw that adults were connecting with them in meaningful ways, the more invested they became in their learning and the more emotionally secure they felt, which resulted in improved achievement.

The Ten- and Two-Minute Intervention

The purpose of the activity is to develop and improve relationships between teachers and students. It can also help to increase levels of engagement with an unmotivated student.

Arrange your staff into small teams of teachers who are likely to have daily or semi-regular contact with the same group of students. Teams can take the following steps:

1. Identify a list of ten students with whom they want to establish a connection or relationship. (Note that the number can be changed in accordance with the size of the school; however, no more than ten is recommended.) While *all* students should feel that connection with at least one teacher at school, the teams can begin with students who have the greatest need for connection.

2. Commit to touching base with two students on the list for ten days using specific requirements for contact ("I noticed . . ." comments such as "I noticed that you almost always wear an NFL jacket," "I noticed that you never go anywhere without your computer," or "I noticed that the people around you are always laughing.") Make no judgments, just observations. Teachers can ask the student about anything, as long as it meets proper moral and ethical guidelines. They should not initiate discussion about the students' difficulties, such as poor classroom motivation, behavioral issues, or lack of engagement. This is a time for teachers to get to know students and students to get to know the teacher without any additional expectations. If a student wishes to talk about what the teacher noticed about him or her, the teacher can respond by revealing something about him- or herself, such as "My son likes the Giants, too," or "I like to paint in my spare time as well." This lets the student know that the interaction is meaningful, a real conversation as opposed to an interrogation.

3. Reconnect as a team to share specific anecdotal notes about communication with the students. Note progress and share feedback and strategies.

4. After ten days, team members evaluate the progress made with each student and determine whether or not to commit to ten more days with one or both students or to add a new student to the system.

Source: Heflebower (2011).

Fostering Close Relationships With Peers

Educators know that relationships with peers are of paramount importance to students. In fact, many times students are so focused on those connections that there is little room for academic pursuits. It may even seem that the job of teachers and administrators is not to foster these connections, but to remove the distraction of them so that students can more readily focus on what they are being asked to learn. However, the critical importance of these peer relationships in a caring learning community is exactly why educators must focus on doing what they can to set the stage for those relationships to be positive, supportive ones. Supporting positive behavior and reducing problem behavior, such as bullying, greatly contributes to building positive relationships among students and creating an emotionally and physically safe environment in which learning can occur.

In addition, leaders can build a caring learning community by helping students fill their need for a sense of belonging and closeness to others through involvement in extracurricular activities at the school or in the community. Mike Petrilli (2008) notes that activities give students "the confidence to achieve in myriad ways—a taste of achievement they then carry into the world of work" (p. 2). Petrilli also indicates that extracurricular activities correlate with a stronger social self-concept. He notes that extracurricular activities benefit students by allowing them to:

- Set goals and work toward them

- Collaborate

- Speak publicly

- Organize their time effectively

- Design and lead projects and teams

- Listen to the concerns of others

- Compete against others

- Juggle multiple tasks

At the elementary level, schools can offer recreation programs, publications, or performing arts projects, hobby or interest clubs, sports teams, or academic clubs such as speech and debate. Extracurricular activities provide students with a network of peers and adults who enjoy similar interests.

It is important to note that offering such activities can be difficult for some schools. Budget was a concern at one school in which I worked. Because of this, several of our activities started at a very small scale. However, the energy generated from these activities encouraged others to become involved. For example, staff members donated their time and energy to begin a running club, a chess club, and a mentoring group for girls called Sister 2 Sister. In a similar effort, I teamed up with a fifth-grade teacher and the physical education teacher to form a boys mentoring group, Boys to Men. By either modeling directly or providing resources, a school principal can lead the effort in increasing the number of extracurricular clubs and activities available to students.

Encouraging Celebration

Schools can help build a caring community by developing meaningful traditions that reach beyond the classroom and create a positive sense of the school as a whole. Schoolwide activities such as sporting events, ceremonies, and assemblies can instill a sense of connectedness and school pride in students. Meaningful celebration provides the opportunity for high-leverage "culture shaping" in which students receive sincere, authentic, and aligned positive feedback. Leaders often overlook alignment in their celebration when celebration lacks a focus on the big picture. In other words, schools celebrate because it feels good. Leaders fail to align celebration with the overarching improvement goals of the school. According to Richard DuFour, Rebecca DuFour, Robert Eaker, & Thomas Many (2010), celebration has its greatest positive impact when:

- The purpose of celebration is made clear.

- The celebration is aligned with student learning.

- There is opportunity for many winners.

For example, many elementary schools use schoolwide assemblies as a stage for student performances. Leaders can use these same assemblies to further build a caring community by highlighting evidence of learning and positive growth toward student achievement of desired goals, reinforcing expectations for positive behavior and student achievement.

Promoting Parent Involvement

A caring learning community welcomes the involvement of parents and community members as partners in their students' education. Many parents and family members today are busy and stressed, some have language barriers, and some are resistant to being involved in their children's schools because they had negative school experiences themselves (Jeynes, 2010). Fully integrating parents and family members into the caring school community may not be as easy as simply asking them to take part in parent programs or to stay in contact with teachers. So how can a principal best welcome parents and family members and encourage their contributions toward a caring learning community? The following methods (Boyer, 1995; Lickona, 1991; Moles, 1996) are simple, but often underutilized:

- *Help parents understand the school's programs and policies.* A home-school handbook provides parents with information about the school, including items such as a statement of school goals, discipline policies, procedures regarding grades and absences, parent-involvement policies, and a calendar of major school events throughout the year. A school-parent contract—a voluntary agreement between the home and school that defines goals, expectations, and shared responsibilities of schools and parents—is another approach that clarifies expectations.

- *Establish regular contact between the home and school.* When educators include parents in goal setting along with their children, they extend to parents the responsibilities of members of a caring learning community. Set up conferences with parents early in the school year and reach out to them often in emails and newsletters or on the school website.

- *Encourage continual contact between parents and family members and teachers and administrators.* This might mean encouraging teachers to share good news through phone calls or emails. Coaches and school counselors can take part in this communication as well. Principals can model the behavior they want to see by taking the time to learn about students' accomplishments and making personal phone calls as well.

- *Encourage supportive contact between parents and their children.* Principals can educate teachers on strategies that encourage familial communication. For example, teachers might prompt students to write down two things they accomplished in one week and one thing they are still working on and show it to their families. They might also ask students to write down a goal on a postcard at the beginning of a grading period and then mail the card home at the end of the period so that family members and students can discuss progress on that goal. Carol Davis and Alice Yang (2009) recommend a class newsletter—"a weekly or biweekly paper bulletin sent home with students—as a tried-and-true communication channel. One way to enrich this strategy is by including a section with a series of "ask me about" questions that parents can use to quiz their children about what they have been learning. This gets students to review important material, clues parents in on the curriculum, and initiates good parent-child conversations" (p. 64).

- *Involve parents as educators at home.* To accomplish this goal, many teachers meet with parents at the beginning of the year and describe homework expectations, encourage parents to read with their children every day, and talk about the power of television as a positive or negative educational tool. In addition, teachers might send home ideas for family games and other informal learning activities throughout the school year.

- *Develop systems for reporting academic and behavioral progress more frequently.* When schools communicate student progress on a frequent basis, staff can intervene more quickly and effectively on the student's behalf. These frequent updates serve almost as a tune-up, a time to stop and assess the effectiveness of strategies, communication, and instruction. To involve parents who have limited English skills, translate information that the school sends home and develop enrichment programs or English-language training programs.

Tips for Parent Contact

Davis and Yang (2009, p. 64) offer tips for administrators and teachers on the art of handling regular contact with parents:

- Make observational notes about students during the week and draw on them later to communicate with parents.

- Start small so you won't get overwhelmed; contact just a few parents at first.

- Work on finding positive things to say about all students, even those who are the most challenging. Students don't need to be perfect to earn a compliment from their teacher.

- Keep telling parents you're open to hearing from them about how to make things better for their children.

In addition to the more traditional strategies, principals can employ the following methods to fully integrate parents and family members into a caring learning community:

- *Treat parents and family members as customers.* Remind teachers and staff that parents and family members are more than simply the people their students go home to—they are customers. William H. Jeynes (2010) notes that parents need to be treated with respect and dignity.

- *Establish and communicate high student expectations to parents and family members.* Both teachers and principals can communicate, through letters, phone calls, home visits, and school events, the high behavioral and academic expectations they set for students. When parents understand these high expectations, they can help support students' drive toward higher achievement.

- *Establish and communicate high expectations for parents and families.* Just as students will rise to the challenges put forth by high expectations, so will parents and family members. Each community is unique, and school staff can collaborate to discover how parents and family members can best contribute to the school community and then clearly communicate those expectations.

Creating a Positive and Welcoming School Building

As a principal, I led an urban school in a community with a high level of poverty. Ours was an older school facility that had fallen into disrepair. In addition to the deterioration that naturally occurs in the life cycle of a building, there was significant neglect both inside and outside of the school. Drab, barren, or dirty school facilities are not places in which students can experience emotional security. It is difficult to establish a caring learning community in such an environment. School budgets are rarely flush with cash, so leaders must focus on cost-effective improvements that often require more elbow grease than funds.

- *Make cleanliness—both inside and outside of the building—a priority.* A clean building does not require additional money in the budget, and it sends a clear message to students, staff, and parents that the school is a welcoming environment. Meet with custodial staff to clarify expectations, and offer support and resources to help staff meet those expectations. Our district had no plans to build a new facility for us anytime soon, so we did the best with what we had and made the best of the building we occupied.

- *Maintain the appearance of the school grounds.* Curb appeal—how school grounds look from the outside—can have a significant impact on the connection students and other members of the school community feel to the school. The grounds surrounding our school, and especially in front of the school, were unkempt. There was trash, and weeds grew between cracks in the sidewalk. Bushes were rarely trimmed. Ask for parent or staff volunteers, call on a local church group, or work with students to help with upkeep. Curb appeal is another improvement that doesn't have to break the budget.

- *Principals should also consider the message people get when they walk through their halls.* Does the focus on high academic expectations and a caring learning environment come through? Consider James M. Kouzes and Barry Z. Posner's (1999) challenge set forth in their book, *Encouraging the Heart: A Leader's Guide to Rewarding and Recognizing Others* (1st ed.):

  > Walk around your facility and examine the images that are on the walls. Are they images that communicate positive messages or negative ones? . . . Do whatever you can to change the images to positive ones. When images are positive, cultures and organizations are in ascendance. (p. 57)

- *Initiate meetings in which staff members discuss the importance of the messages students and community members see on school walls.* Do they communicate clearly that learning is the fundamental purpose of the school? Do walls showcase colorful and engaging displays of authentic student work? Hallways should be mirrors for students; they should see themselves as they walk through the school. The goal should be for any member of the school community—and especially students—to see promise and possibility within the halls of the building. For many students, school is the safest and most stable institution in their lives. Thus, it is critical for principals to do all they can to create a positive and welcoming physical environment.

Summary

Students cannot feel emotionally safe and secure in an environment that lacks a strong foundation. The principal plays an important role in creating a strong foundation by building a caring learning environment in which students feel valued and respected. These learning environments are welcoming physical spaces that develop student initiative by creating both high academic and behavioral expectations, that develop resilience in students, help them develop close relationships with adults and peers, encourage celebration, and promote parental involvement.

2

Helping Students Deal With Conflict and Anger

Educators have long understood that behavior difficulties can keep students from functioning productively in class. . . . The relationship between behavior and learning must not only be considered but acted upon.

—MARY MAGEE QUINN, ROBERT A. GABLE,
ROBERT B. RUTHERFORD, JR., C. MICHAEL NELSON,
AND KENNETH W. HOWELL

Even in typically peaceful schools, students will experience conflict and anger. Their ability to deal with difficult issues and the emotions that ensue affects not only their personal well-being but also the climate and safety of the entire school. Research has found that schools with orderly, safe environments, in which conflicts are resolved cooperatively and fairly, generally have higher levels of student achievement (Payne, Connoy, & Racine, 1998; Stockard & Mayberry, 1992). Therefore, in the interest of preserving a community conducive to learning, schools must address the issue of what to do when conflict and anger arise.

If students have the skills to deal with conflict and anger constructively, the goal of a peaceful and positive school climate in which learning can occur is more likely to be reached. This chapter examines factors that place students at risk for experiencing high levels of conflict or reacting to conflict violently, and it offers strategies for helping students deal productively with anger and for establishing a schoolwide culture of peaceful and fair conflict resolution.

The Roots of Conflict and Anger

Conflict can be a positive force, leading to personal growth, learning, the discovery of new alternatives, and social change—if the people involved feel that they have the ability to cooperate with one another and come up with creative solutions that will preserve and even enhance their relationships. Too often, however, conflict can lead to anger. Angry students feel isolated and alone, unable to establish a dialogue with their peers and unwilling to enlist the help of adults in settling their differences. Confronted with feelings of loneliness, frustration, and powerlessness, angry students may be propelled toward acts of disruption or violence. Researchers (Federman, 1998; Johnson & Johnson, 1995a; Remboldt, 1998) have identified a number of societal trends that put all children at greater risk for experiencing high levels of conflict and anger, including the following:

- Changing patterns of family life such as greater isolation from overworked parents, divorce, abuse, and poverty

- Changing patterns of community life as society has redefined violence as the norm rather than the exception, and young people have gained easier access to guns and drugs

- Desensitization to violence due to the frequency of violent images in the media

In addition, certain factors in a student's background may put him or her at risk for experiencing high levels of anger or behaving violently (Guetzloe & Rockwell, 1998; Hartzell & Petrie, 1992; Sabatino, 1997). These include:

- Poor modeling of anger management by parents or other adult authority figures

- Inadequate parental management marked by inconsistent or harsh discipline or lack of supervision

- High levels of psychological pathology within the child or parent

Although societal and family conditions are beyond the control of schools, school leaders and other educators *do* have control over establishing a school climate that is supportive and protective of every student. This is a worthy goal, though it is one that has become increasingly difficult in contemporary society.

There was a time when concern over conflict and anger was primarily reserved for schools with high poverty in urban areas. Having been a leader at schools nestled in the suburbs and schools in high-poverty areas, I have seen firsthand that, to differing degrees, all schools experience challenges with conflict and anger. As a principal, one of my biggest challenges was helping staff members understand and embrace the fact that we had control over establishing the desired school environment and culture—including helping curb conflict and anger among students. This proved to be a very daunting task in the midst of a cycle of academic failure and the myriad of challenges that come along with that. The issues students brought with them to school seemed overwhelming. Conflict and anger were significant concerns in our school, so we focused on reinforcing positive school climate while simultaneously focusing on moving toward academic excellence.

Integrating Conflict-Management Strategies Into the School Culture

Many schools have attempted to reduce conflict among students through violence prevention programs. Unfortunately, these programs do not always work (Posner, 1994). Researchers offer several factors that lead to failure in some of these programs: they provide brief training and materials without adequate follow-up; they underestimate the strength of the social forces that cause children to behave violently; and their interventions tend to be crisis oriented, occurring only after violent patterns have been well-established (Clarke & Campbell, 1998; Johnson & Johnson, 1995b).

Even a well-designed violence prevention program is likely to be ineffective if it is presented as an add-on or as an isolated lesson. Research suggests that the most effective approach is to integrate conflict management and violence prevention strategies into the school culture. A comprehensive approach, one that creates a profound change in school culture, is needed because "ultimately peer groups, not individuals, promote an ethic of aggression" (Labi, 2001).

Schools successful in conflict management foster norms against violence, aggression, and bullying. They cultivate an attitude of respect and caring for others, reinforcing for students that violence is not the norm. Successful schools also focus on providing students with concrete skills training, such as anger management and media resistance, to help them avoid destructive influences.

To reduce the frequency of interpersonal aggression and curb conflict and anger, research supports taking a whole-school approach. According to Jim Larson (2008):

> This approach recognizes that everyone in the building, staff members and students alike, contributes to an environment that either increases or decreases the likelihood of student aggression and involves prevention efforts that address the needs of everyone. The objective is to create an environment that decreases the likelihood of aggressive behavior while increasing the opportunities for learning socially desirable conflict resolution and anger management strategies. (p. 13)

The Role of Students

As members of a caring learning community, students play an important role in the establishment and maintenance of a peaceful school. Interventions should focus on helping students develop techniques so they can manage their anger to avoid conflict and deal with their anger in healthy and productive ways (Horton, 1996; Kreidler, 1996; Sabatino, 1997; Studer, 1996). This training should help students understand that an important part of membership in a caring community is looking out for and reaching out to their peers, and they should be encouraged to discuss their concerns about their peers with their parents, teachers, and other members of the school community. Training in self-management, anger management, and positive decision making should not be reserved for just some members of the student body, such as the most aggressive students or those with behavior problems. Rather, all children should be instructed in how to understand and deal with their own feelings of anger or powerlessness and given opportunities to direct their own learning. The instruction students receive in self-discipline and anger management can help them identify signs of frustration and anger in their schoolmates as well, thus contributing to an overall culture of emotional and physical safety.

The Role of School Staff

When school leaders, teachers, and other staff members understand the nature of conflict and the factors that contribute to student anger, they are better prepared to help students deal more effectively with their anger and to expose students to alternative, nonviolent approaches to resolving conflict.

School can be difficult for students as they juggle the expectations of the adult world while navigating the pressures of youth culture. They often neglect to share their concerns about themselves or their peers with adults at their school because they fear retribution by and ostracism from peers, and they blame school authorities for not following up on their concerns. Principals can encourage students to discuss their concerns by keeping conversations with students private and confidential, by responding to student input in a timely, discreet, and professional manner, and by establishing this type of behavior as the norm for all adults in the school.

The instruction students receive in self-management and anger management is greatly strengthened when leaders also model responsible ways of dealing with their own anger as it surfaces. Modeling responsible anger management involves expressing anger in direct but nonaggressive ways. For example, a teacher might express his or her anger by saying, "I felt angry this morning when you all misbehaved during the math lesson. By talking to your neighbors instead of paying attention to me, you did not show me respect." This approach both clarifies for the students what caused the teacher to become angry and implicitly identifies the behavior that would have been acceptable. Schools often make the mistake of trying to establish a healthy physical and emotional environment by developing expectations that focus solely on student behaviors. It is critically important that the adults in the school model what they expect from students. We can't have a school culture that has one set of rules for adults and another for students.

Developing Schoolwide Conflict-Management Strategies

A variety of schoolwide strategies can promote a peaceful school culture and equip students to manage their conflict and anger constructively. Children who are at high risk for violence, academic failure, and dropping out of school often lack a connection to a positive social group such as a family, peer group, or church (Posner, 1994). By developing an infrastructure that supports long-term, caring relationships between students and their peers and teachers, schools can combat feelings of isolation.

Strategies for Conflict Resolution

Conflicts between students do occur. Principals can provide students with strategies to resolve these conflicts. According to Richard J. Bodine and Donna K. Crawford (1998):

- The use of conflict-resolution strategies can improve the school climate and thus help to reduce violence and chronic school absence.

- Conflict resolution training improves important life skills for students, such as listening, critical thinking, problem solving, and perspective taking.

- Shifting the responsibility for resolving some conflicts to students frees up time for teachers to focus on instruction rather than discipline.

They also offer four principles that serve as the foundation for successful conflict-resolution programs:

1. *Separate people from the problem.* Before working on a substantive problem, students should disentangle relationship issues and deal with them separately. Rather than taking things personally, students should see themselves as attacking the problem, not each other.

2. *Focus on interests, not positions.* Students should focus on what they really want (that is, their underlying interests), rather than on the positions they hold. They should seek to reconcile their interests rather than to compromise between positions. This approach works because for every interest there are usually several satisfactory solutions.

3. *Invent options for mutual gain.* This approach gives students the opportunity to brainstorm potential solutions that advance shared interests without the constraint of finding a single answer or the pressure of deciding immediately. An important ground rule is for students to postpone criticism and judgment until they have produced many possible options for reconciling their differences.

4. *Use objective criteria.* Neither student should have to "give in" to the other; rather, the resolution must be objective and based on fair standards and procedures. Invite the students to state the reasoning behind their preferred solution to the conflict, suggest objective criteria that apply, and insist that the conflict be resolved on the basis of those criteria.

Strategies for Problem Solving

Three problem-solving strategies are very useful with students: negotiation, mediation, and consensus decision making (Bodine & Crawford, 1998). In *negotiation*, students meet face-to-face and work together, without assistance, to resolve their dispute. *Mediation* differs from negotiation in that the students are joined by a mediator, a neutral third party who resolves the dispute (this strategy is discussed in the next section in further detail). *Consensus decision making* is a group problem-solving process in which all students meet to collaboratively develop a plan of action to resolve a dispute; it may or may not be facilitated by a mediator.

Schools can also use controversy for instructional purposes. This strategy is called *academic controversy.* To implement this approach, the teacher selects an issue for discussion, places students in cooperative learning groups, and assigns students positions to advocate through organizing information and deriving conclusions. Students then present their positions, challenge one another's positions, and search for additional information to view the issue from both perspectives simultaneously. This approach has been found to enhance students' social support and self-esteem, as well as provide academic benefits. However, the benefits of academic controversy are realized only if they occur in a cooperative, noncompetitive context (Johnson & Johnson, 1995a).

Mediating Conflicts

Modeling a consistent conflict resolution process for use by students is critical to creating a physically and emotionally safe environment and to teaching students how to properly manage their anger. Audrey Quinlan (2004) outlines a step-by-step protocol used by one veteran principal for mediating student conflicts, such as fights, verbal harassment, and so on. Although using this type of procedure to talk through problems takes a lot of time, it pays off by giving students tools they can use to mediate their own conflicts.

1. Separate the students and ask them to write down what happened. This helps defuse their anger and provides documentation of the conflict. Read what students wrote, and ask them for clarification if necessary.

2. Bring the students together and tell them you will work together to find a solution that's agreeable to both of them (no winner or loser).

3. Explain and get agreement on the ground rules for the mediation:

   › Talk only to the principal.

   › Take turns talking.

   › Stay seated.

   › Don't interrupt.

   › Keep what is said confidential.

4. Ask the students who wants to go first and allow that student to explain the conflict. Next, give the other student the same opportunity. In this phase, the students should look each other in the eye and talk honestly about how the conflict made them feel.

5. Brainstorm possible ways to ensure that the conflict will never happen again, including wacky and impossible ideas. The ultimate solution is usually somewhere on the list.

6. Help students choose and agree on the best solution, write up a contract that lists the terms of their agreement, have both students sign it, and make copies for everyone. Thank the students for participating.

Just as principals can encourage students to deal positively with issues of conflict and anger, the same can be done for teachers and other staff members. I remember many incidents as a school leader when I had to address adult behaviors that weren't aligned with the culture we agreed to create. Confronting those issues involves providing modeling, giving gentle reminders, and making adults aware of their poor choices. Whether conflicts with teachers are large or small, the principal has to be willing to model the behaviors set up to create a caring community and be willing to protect and defend the culture when students and adults alike threaten it.

Training in *peer mediation*—where students mediate their own disputes or the disputes of other students—typically occurs in two steps:

1. *Negotiation training*—Students learn to define the conflict, exchange positions and suggestions, view the situation from both perspectives, come up with options for mutual gain, and reach a satisfactory agreement. Students need to over-learn these skills so that they become automatic—even when they are experiencing feelings of fear and anger.

2. *Conflict mediation*—Students learn how to mediate resolutions to the conflicts of their classmates.

There are two basic models for peer mediation: (1) the total school model, in which the entire school is trained in mediation and each student has the opportunity to function as a mediator, and (2) the student club model, in which students are selected from the entire student body to receive mediation training and function as mediators.

The advantage of the total school model is that all students receive instruction in how to resolve conflicts constructively and reinforce their skills through acting as a mediator. When using the student club model, leaders must take care to select students in a way that represents the diversity of the student body. That is, the pool of mediators should include students from at-risk populations and those who traditionally do not get involved in school activities (Lupton-Smith et al., 1996).

One example of the club model comes from an elementary school in Idaho where the student conflict-resolution team is made up of students from various grades. These students mediate problems at recess. According to the playground supervisor, there has been a marked difference in the way students interact on the playground since the establishment of this cross-grade partnership: "All of the kids seem to find more to do and the younger kids aren't as intimidated by the older kids. Some of the older students even seem protective of their younger buddies" (Youngerman, 1998, pp. 58, 60).

Principals can also develop a classroom-based mediation model. First, an entire class is trained in the use of mediation skills. Then, the teacher selects two class members each day to serve as official mediators. If a conflict that arises that day cannot be resolved by the disputants, it is referred to one of the class mediators (Johnson, Johnson, Dudley, & Barnett, 1992).

Five Major Areas of Conflict

Student mediators in one school identified five major areas of conflict (Robinson, Smith, & Daunic, 2000, pp. 25-26):

1. Minor issues such as arguments over inconsequential topics or "having a bad day"
2. Personal attacks such as picking on or insulting another student and spreading rumors
3. Social skill deficits such as failure to see another's viewpoint, inability to communicate, or inability to control one's temper

continued →

4. Typical student issues such as disputes with parents about chores and boyfriend/girlfriend issues

5. Status issues such as attempting to boost one's reputation through self-aggrandizement or exaggeration

Modeling De-escalation

When students are angry there is always the possibility that they can become aggressive. Principals should develop de-escalation procedures to defuse potentially problematic situations with students. It is wise to teach these procedures to staff members and practice them using role play. Larson (2008, p. 13) suggests the following strategies for de-escalation:

- Reduce the student's potential to engage in face-saving aggression by removing any peer spectators.

- Take a nonthreatening stance with your body at an angle to the student and your empty hands at your sides in plain sight.

- Maintain a calm demeanor and steady, level voice, even in the face of intense verbal disrespect or threats from the student.

- Acknowledge the student's emotional condition empathetically—for example, "You're really angry, and I want to understand why."

- Control the interaction by setting limits—such as, "I want you to sit down before we continue" or "We can talk, but only if you stop swearing."

- Provide problem-solving counseling with a school psychologist or counselor at the earliest opportunity.

Fostering Parental Involvement

Parental involvement is an important component in helping students constructively manage their conflict and anger. Students benefit when educators and parents work together to develop a caring learning community in which conflicts are dealt with constructively. Researchers Mark R. Warren, Soo Hong, Carolyn Leung Rubin, and Phitsamay Sychitkokhong Uy (2009) note that the connection many schools in low-income areas have with parents and the surrounding community is weak. They note that "in these schools, a few brave souls become active and involved. . . . But most urban schools fail to engage families broadly and deeply around the education of their children" (p. 2). Too frequently, contact between school and home only occurs when conflict has already escalated to the point that it has caused social or academic problems. When school leaders and parents work together consistently they can help students handle conflict in constructive ways, minimize anger issues, and deal with anger in healthy ways when it does arise.

Summary

Dealing with conflict publicly and collectively is an integral part of a caring learning community. Collectively addressing issues of conflict and anger is first and foremost a safety concern, but it also helps students develop skills for conflict and anger management. Through constructive conflict resolution, students develop good judgment, self-discipline, problem-solving abilities, and the benefits of understanding the perspectives of others, which are essential life skills that they can draw on throughout their school years and beyond.

Developing an Effective Schoolwide Behavior and Discipline Plan

Proactive, school-wide approaches are considered best practice in addressing the challenge of maintaining discipline.

—RICHARD WHITE, BOB ALGOZZINE, ROBERT AUDETTE, MARY BETH MARR, AND EDWARD D. ELLIS, JR.

The main goals of school discipline are to ensure the safety of staff and students and to create an environment conducive to learning. Research has found that a safe and orderly environment and effective classroom management are two of the most important factors affecting student achievement (Marzano, Pickering, & Heflebower, 2011). While the importance of effective behavior management is clear, it is not always easy for principals to define their roles in making this happen. Traditionally, the principal's role has been to manage from within his or her office: handling discipline when a teacher no longer feels capable. Not surprisingly, this strategy is often not effective except in the most serious cases, and it leads to a buildingwide view of the principal as an unapproachable authoritarian. In a caring learning community, the principal leads his or her staff in creating an effective schoolwide behavior and discipline plan that involves specific strategies for communication within problem situations and the uniform implementation of focused, consistent rewards and consequences so that students feel emotionally and physically safe.

Discipline in a Caring Learning Community

In most cases, problematic behavior in school is not, in and of itself, an insurmountable problem. As the Learning First Alliance (2001) notes:

> Eighty percent of students come to school able to learn, conform to rules, and follow ordinary social conventions. Another 15 percent, on average, are able to fit in and succeed with modest additional assistance, such as conflict resolution or emotion-management training. The remaining 5 percent or so engage in severe and chronic problem behaviors and need more intensive and ongoing help, such as regular individual counseling or placement in alternative programs that provide greater supervision, structure, and support. (p. 14)

In other words, most students are both willing and able to be productive members of caring learning communities; however, no school is perfect, and student behavior issues will inevitably arise. What is critical is not whether the issues arise, but rather how school leaders and staff deal with them. The typical problem with schools' approaches to discipline is that it is piecemeal. A schoolwide approach to behavior and discipline is more effective since it is consistent, recognizes positive behavior, and works to stop inappropriate behaviors. In addition, it creates a culture of recognition that allows students to monitor their own behavior so they are not misbehaving to get attention (Brownell & Walther-Thomas, 1999). When schools approach behavior-management issues as a community, they avoid isolated, ineffective results. A key part of developing a caring learning community is creating and communicating a schoolwide behavior and discipline plan that spells out policies for appropriate behavior.

Establishing Schoolwide Behavior Expectations

The defining feature of an effective schoolwide behavior and discipline plan is a focus on schoolwide behavior expectations. These are behaviors educators want students to display. This approach is different from the traditional focus on eliminating undesirable behaviors. Placing effort and focus on those behaviors we want to see repeated over and over again allows those behaviors to grow. This is not to say that leaders should ignore or not address undesirable behavior; however, the primary focus in a caring learning community should be on promoting and establishing expected behaviors. These expectations should be limited in number as to not overwhelm students, and they should be applicable in all school settings. Figure 3.1 shows a sample of schoolwide behavior expectations from Broad Acres Elementary in Silver Spring, Maryland. Figure 3.2 shows expectations from Evoline C. West Elementary in Fairburn, Georgia.

1. **B**e respectful
2. **A**ct responsibly
3. **R**emain ready
4. **K**eep safe

Source: Broad Acres Elementary. Reprinted with permission.

Figure 3.1: Sample schoolwide expectations.

Show Your Wildcat P.R.I.D.E!

✓ **P**repared for school

✓ **R**espectful to self and others

✓ **I**n charge of my words and actions

✓ **D**irect my ears and eyes to the speaker

✓ **E**arn and give praise

Source: Evoline C. West Elementary. Reprinted with permission.

Figure 3.2: Sample schoolwide expectations.

The following guidelines will help school staffs identify and develop schoolwide behavioral expectations:

1. Establish a process for identifying behavioral expectations, such as a leadership team that develops a draft that is then taken to the faculty for discussion, revision, and adoption.

2. Limit the number of behavioral expectations to no more than five.

3. State the behavioral expectations in positive, action-based terms using simple, understandable language.

4. Identify specific desirable behaviors in all school settings.

5. Ensure the language used in the expectations is age appropriate for the students.

6. Ensure the expectations can be applied in academic and social situations.

Students need clear expectations about how to behave in all settings in the school—in the classroom, library, cafeteria, hallway, and playground. Traditionally, schools have set specific expectations for each setting. This means staff members had to remember the expectations for each setting and do their best to ensure students met those expectations. The value of schoolwide expectations is in their efficiency and simplicity. If the schoolwide expectation is, "Be responsible," then that expectation can then be applied to many settings. For instance, an example of being responsible in the classroom would be to come to class prepared. In the hallways, it would be walking quietly. In the restroom, being responsible means leaving the area clean. There is a common theme of be responsible with specific applications in each setting. A schoolwide behavior expectation chart establishes the expected behaviors in all settings in the school. Figure 3.3 (page 30) shows an example of a chart from Washoe Inspire Academy in Reno, Nevada for "Be respectful."

Be Respectful					
	Playground	Hallway	Classroom	Restroom	Lunch Area
Individuals	Honor personal space. Have appropriate conversations. Treat others the way you want to be treated.	Honor personal space. Have quiet, appropriate conversations.	Honor personal space. Have appropriate conversations at appropriate times.	Honor personal space. Have appropriate conversations.	Have appropriate conversations. Disagree appropriately.
Self	Be on time. Act responsibly. Engage in healthy activities.	Follow the dress code. Walk to the right.	Show your best effort. Follow teacher instructions. Challenge yourself.	Get permission. Practice good hygiene.	Use an appropriate voice and tone. Ask permission to leave your seat.
Environment	Think of safety first. Be graffiti free. Keep school grounds clean.	Think of safety first. Be graffiti free. Keep the hallways clean.	Think of safety first. Let others learn. Be graffiti free.	Think of safety first. Keep the restroom clean. Be graffiti free.	Think of safety first. Keep the eating area clean. Put all trash in the garbage can.

Source: Washoe Inspire Academy. Reprinted with permission.

Figure 3.3: Sample schoolwide behavior expectations chart.

Teaching Behavioral Expectations to Students

In a caring learning community, teaching students the expectations for positive schoolwide behavior is just as important as academic learning; therefore, educators should provide direct instruction to all students in the behavioral expectations. The following are some general guidelines for teaching positive behaviors from the Michigan Department of Education (2010, p. 15):

- *Teach behaviors as you would teach academics or any other skill.* Emphasize the language and terminology. Tell students why it is important. Use demonstration, modeling, and role-playing to teach expectations. Give examples of what good behavior is and what it is not. Make sure students are actively involved in the lesson. Give them opportunities to demonstrate and practice the expected behaviors. Then, over the course of the school year, plan refresher lessons about once a week. In addition, provide lessons to new students or when many students are having difficulty with an expectation.

- *Keep lessons brief.* Lessons should be five to fifteen minutes. Providing frequent, brief lessons is more effective than providing a few long lessons that might not keep student attention and engagement.

- *Take students to various locations in the school for instruction.* Ideally, the staff responsible for supervising students in a specific setting should be involved in teaching the expected behavior in that setting.

- *All adults should have awareness and be invested.* All adults in the school should be aware of the behavior expectations and take every opportunity to model the behaviors.

Students learn best by doing. If leaders want positive behavior results, they must take the time to teach the desired behavior. No single poster, chart, assembly, or document alone will embed desired behaviors into a school's culture; deep implementation requires teaching, learning, and practicing.

Reinforcing and Rewarding Positive Behaviors

Once behavior expectations have been taught, staff members need to take additional steps to assist students in exhibiting the expected behaviors on a consistent basis over time. If leaders, teachers, and all school staff do not reinforce and reward appropriate behavior, it is highly likely that some—if not many—students will discontinue displaying appropriate behaviors, and problem behaviors are sure to emerge. The following strategies are helpful for reinforcing and rewarding appropriate behavior:

- *Be a positive role model.* The adults in a school serve as significant role models for their students when they show respect and courtesy to others, encourage their students, solve problems in a calm and respectful manner, show empathy and concern for them when needed, and are firm, fair, and consistent.

- *Continually reinforce positive behavioral expectations.* Reinforcement is very effective for establishing behavioral expectations and creating a welcoming and supportive school environment. Staff should frequently acknowledge students who demonstrate expected behavior and provide constant reminders, supervision, and feedback when students do not follow expectations. There should be a strong emphasis on students self-directing their behavior.

Schools often focus too much attention on problem behaviors. The reinforcement of expected behaviors is equally as important. When teachers and other staff members pay attention to the students who display the desired behaviors rather than those who cause disruption, they provide an incentive for students to achieve behavioral expectations.

A schoolwide recognition plan is one way schools can develop rewards that are accessible to *all* students; opportunities for all students to achieve success are critically important. An effective schoolwide recognition plan does the following (adapted from Colvin, 2007):

- Specify which schoolwide behavior expectations you will acknowledge.

- Identify a staff member to coordinate the award process.

- Give the award a title.

- Define the eligibility criteria.

- Determine where and when to present the award and what the actual award will be that is given to the student.

- Decide how to display and communicate the recognition to others in the school and community.

- Determine the frequency of the recognition.

Laying the Groundwork

It is important for leaders to lay the groundwork with faculty before implementing a system of rewards and recognition. Some staff members may oppose these plans—they might see them as rewarding students for what they should be doing anyway or bribing students to do the right thing. Leaders must emphasize that students need recognition to reinforce positive behavior, and that the focus should be on showing appreciation—not simply on distributing rewards.

At Broad Acres Elementary, students can earn BARK tickets from their teachers as rewards for positive behavior that make them eligible for various prizes and opportunities for special recognition throughout the school year. Figure 3.4 shows the details of the BARK incentive program.

School staff often complain that they spend too much time focused on students who exhibit problem behavior. Consequently, students who cooperate with the expectations and behave appropriately at school receive very little of their time. Caring learning communities that have a schoolwide recognition plan in place ensure that students who consistently meet behavior expectations receive recognition and attention for their efforts. A plan such as this is one of the surest strategies for sustaining desirable behaviors schoolwide. The effectiveness of a recognition plan is largely determined by the willingness of the staff to implement the details with high levels of commitment and consistency.

Addressing Challenging Behaviors

Addressing challenging behaviors is one of the most difficult aspects of a schoolwide behavior and discipline plan to implement effectively in schools. Addressing challenging behaviors inappropriately can lead to an ongoing cycle of student problem behavior and punishment. The traditional way to deal with challenging behaviors in education is to punish, and if the problem behavior recurs, then deliver more intense punishment, and so the cycle continues. In a caring learning community with a proactive approach to schoolwide discipline, staff members do more than just deliver negative consequences; they assist students in learning how to behave appropriately in the future. A proactive model for effectively correcting problem behaviors includes a system of responses for managing challenging behaviors, both in the classroom and in the office.

Daily, grades k–5: Teachers provide a wide variety of daily incentives (including BARK tickets) based on their individual styles and student needs.

Monthly, grades k–5: Students who have received twenty or more tickets will be randomly selected to spin the BARK wheel during lunch.

Grades k–2: Twenty students per grade will be randomly picked monthly.

Grades 3–5: Ten students per grade will be randomly picked monthly.

Monthly, grades k–5: Five students per grade will be selected to attend a BARK breakfast hosted by the administration for students who received twenty or more tickets.

Quarterly, grades 1–5: At the end of each quarter, students who have earned fifty or more BARK tickets during each marking period will be eligible for the random drawing of a new bike and helmet (one boy and one girl).

Semester, grades 3, 4, 5: At the end of each semester, students with 100 BARK tickets (first semester) and 200 BARK tickets (second semester) will be invited to the BARK disco.

Bulldog Star, grades k–5: Students will get their picture and name on the Bulldog wall of fame and receive a "Be a Star" t-shirt after earning 200 BARK tickets.

End of Year, grades 2, 3, 4, 5: Students that have earned 300 or more BARK tickets will be eligible for a drawing to attend a special end-of-year grand prize drawing for a limo ride, bowling, and lunch during school. Ten students will win.

Source: Broad Acres Elementary. Reprinted with permission.

Figure 3.4: The BARK incentive program.

In order to create a safe and secure learning environment for students, leaders and staff must work together to determine when problem behaviors should be handled by staff and when administration needs to intervene. Cotton (1995) found this to be the most divisive issue between staff and administration. It is critical for school leaders and staff to be clear on what behaviors will be handled by administration through office referrals and what teachers can handle in the classroom.

Behaviors that should be handled by the office typically include physical fighting or violence, serious disruption, behaviors that compromise school safety, and potentially illegal behavior. In most cases, leaders can align the school's list of office-referral behaviors with the district policy, which typically dictates serious behaviors and infractions. Figure 3.5 (page 34) shows a sample of behaviors for which teachers should issue office referrals.

Once staff has reached agreement on the list of behaviors that should result in an office referral, the next step is to develop the definitions for each of these behaviors. The definitions will help staff

- Fighting or assault
- Property damage or vandalism
- Leaving school grounds without permission
- Possession of weapons
- Possession of illegal substances
- Forgery or theft
- Persistent disruptive behavior
- Harassment and bullying

Source: Adapted from Todd, Horner, and Tobin (2007).

Figure 3.5: Sample list of office-referral behaviors.

to be consistent in assessing whether to make an office referral. This is a critical step in the process. Without a common language, staff members will likely have different interpretations of each behavior. These definitions should be shared with parents as well to support effective communication. Table 3.1 shows sample definitions for office-referral behaviors developed at one school.

Table 3.1: Sample Definitions for Office-Referral Behaviors

Behavior	Definition
Fighting or assault	Student uses actions involving serious physical contact where injury may occur (such as hitting, punching, hitting with an object, kicking, hair pulling, scratching, and so on).
Property damage or vandalism	Student participates in an activity that results in destruction or disfigurement of property.
Leaving school grounds without permission	Student is in an area that is outside of school boundaries (as defined by school).
Possession of weapons	Student is in possession of knives or guns (real or fake) or other objects readily capable of causing bodily harm.
Possession of illegal substances	Student is in possession of or is using illegal drugs, substances, or imitations.
Forgery or theft	Student is in possession of, has passed on, or is responsible for removing someone else's property or has signed a person's name without that person's permission.
Persistent disruptive behavior	Student has refused to follow directions, is talking back, or exhibits socially rude interactions.
Harassment or bullying	Student delivers disrespectful messages (verbal or with gestures) to another person that include threats and intimidation, obscene gestures, pictures, or written notes. Disrespectful messages include negative comments based on race, religion, gender, age, or national origin; and sustained or intense verbal attacks based on ethnic origin, disabilities, or other personal matters.

Source: Adapted from Todd, Horner, and Tobin (2007).

It is critical for the administration to receive thorough and comprehensive information from teachers so that situations involving challenging behavior can be dealt with and processed appropriately. Office referral forms should be designed to meet the following needs:

- Provide administration with the critical information to process the problem.

- Allow for some level of data entry into an online tracking system.

- Allow administration to track consequences and actions taken.

- Inform the referring staff member of the actions taken.

The form should include such information as the location of the event, possible motivation, if others were involved, interventions used, and the administrative resolution. Figure 3.6 (page 36) shows a sample behavior support tracking form from Washoe County School District. Forms can also be designed for students to self-assess their behaviors. Figure 3.7 (page 37) shows a form used by Broad Acres Elementary for students in grades 3 through 5.

While the office referral spells out those behavioral offenses that administration will address, staff is expected to manage the problem behaviors that are not listed on the office referral. While these behaviors are often called "minor behaviors," it is still very important that there is a systems approach for addressing and correcting these behaviors. If not, the behaviors may worsen and may negatively affect the positive learning environment teachers are trying to establish and maintain. For example, if a student doesn't come to class prepared and this behavior persists, then it's not long before the student may refuse to do any of the assigned work. Other students may see this growing pattern of behavior, follow suit, and act out the same way.

Collecting and Using Data

A key to an effective schoolwide behavior and discipline plan is to collect and use data. Far too often, schools determine the success or failure of a program based on intentions rather than measurable results. In order for the plan to be effective, schools must commit not only to collecting data, but using the data to inform their progress and ensure that they are strengthening the emotional and physical security of the school. In addition, the best way to reinforce staff and student commitment to the plan is to show clear and compelling evidence that it is working. The following are steps schools can take for data collection and use:

- Designate a person who is responsible for data entry, and monitor the data entry.

- Pull weekly data reports.

- Report data to staff on a frequent basis.

- Use data to guide decisions.

- Share results with all stakeholders (parents, staff, and students).

Behavior Support Tracking Form

Student Name: _____

Grade Level: _____

Behavior Event #: _____

Staff Member: _____

Date: _____

Time: _____

School: _____

Location of Event

- ☐ Restroom
- ☐ Bus
- ☐ Cafeteria
- ☐ Classroom
- ☐ Common Area
- ☐ Gym
- ☐ Hallway
- ☐ Library
- ☐ Locker room
- ☐ Off campus
- ☐ Office
- ☐ Parking lot
- ☐ Playground
- ☐ Special event
- ☐ Unknown
- ☐ Other

Positive Recognition

- ☐ Academic recognition: _____
- ☐ Positive behavior recognition: _____
- ☐ Award/other: _____

Minor Behavior Event

- ☐ Academic integrity
- ☐ Damage to school property
- ☐ Defiance/disrespect/insubordination
- ☐ Dress code violation
- ☐ Invasion of personal space
- ☐ Inappropriate language
- ☐ Physical aggression
- ☐ Property misuse
- ☐ Tardy
- ☐ Technology violation
- ☐ Other: _____
- ☐ Unknown

Intervention (Staff)

- ☐ Intervention: _____
- ☐ Peer mediation
- ☐ Modify work
- ☐ Verbal cue
- ☐ Positive reinforcement: _____
- ☐ Reteach expectation
- ☐ Student conference
- ☐ Student contract
- ☐ Differentiated instruction
- ☐ Reflection activity
- ☐ Extra time spent on task
- ☐ Referral to intervention assistant team
- ☐ Loss of item/class privilege
- ☐ Focused detention:
  - ☐ Reflection activity
  - ☐ Instructional recovery
  - ☐ Other: _____
- ☐ Conference/contact:
  - ☐ Parent
  - ☐ Student
  - Date: _____
- ☐ Recovery in room
- ☐ Seating change

Possible Motivation

- ☐ Avoid adult(s)
- ☐ Avoid peer(s)
- ☐ Avoid task/activity
- ☐ Obtain adult attention
- ☐ Obtain peer attention
- ☐ Obtain item/activity
- ☐ Other: _____
- ☐ Unknown

Others Involved

- ☐ Peers
- ☐ Staff member
- ☐ Unknown
- ☐ Other: _____

Behavior Resolution (Administration)

- ☐ Referral to Intervention Assistance Team
- ☐ Intervention
- ☐ Tier 2 intervention: _____
- ☐ Check in/check out
- ☐ Tier 2 intervention: _____
- ☐ Conference/contact
  - ☐ Parent
  - ☐ Student
  - Date: _____
- ☐ School beautification
- ☐ Restitution
- ☐ Focused detention
  - ☐ Reflection activity
  - ☐ Instructional recovery
  - ☐ Other: _____
- ☐ In-school suspension
- ☐ BUS
  - ☐ Start date: _____
  - ☐ End date: _____
- ☐ Saturday school date: _____
- ☐ After-school intervention
- ☐ GRIP/SIP/VIP: _____
- ☐ Other admin decision:
  _____

Major Behavior Event

- ☐ Academic integrity
- ☐ Attendance/truancy
- ☐ Damage to school property
- ☐ Defiance/disrespect/insubordination
- ☐ Disturbance of school activities
- ☐ Dress code violation
- ☐ Fighting/physical aggression
- ☐ Gang-related behavior
- ☐ Harassment/bullying/intimidation
- ☐ Possession of alcohol
- ☐ Possession of controlled substance
- ☐ Possession of weapon: _____
- ☐ Sales/distribution of controlled substance
- ☐ Tardy
- ☐ Technology violation
- ☐ Theft
- ☐ Threat to staff
- ☐ Threat to student
- ☐ Tobacco
- ☐ Violence
- ☐ Violence/staff
- ☐ Other: _____

☐ **Additional Comments:**

☐ **Additional Information (See Attached):**

Signatures: _____ / _____ / _____ / _____
Student Signature   Administrator Signature   Parent Signature   Date

Parent notification/signature required after each major event.

Source: Washoe County School District. Reprinted with permission.

Figure 3.6: Sample behavior support tracking form.

BARK Expectation Self-Assessment (Grades 3 to 5)	Parent Signature: _____ Date: _____
	Student: _____
	Date: _____
	Time: _____

1. I need to

Be Respectful   Act Responsibly   Remain Ready   Keep Safe

2. I didn't meet expectations because I wanted:

☐ Attention from an adult   ☐ To avoid doing my school work
☐ Attention from another child   ☐ To be in control of the situation
☐ To make an adult become angry   ☐ Something that someone else had
☐ To let someone know that I am mad at him or her ☐ Other: _____

This is what happened: _____

_____

_____

_____

_____

This is a better choice I can make next time: _____

_____

_____

_____

_____

Student Signature: _____

3. Staff Comments:

☐ Physical assault   ☐ Fighting   ☐ Theft or robbery
☐ Insubordination   ☐ Intimidation   ☐ Vandalism
☐ Verbal abuse   ☐ Weapon possession   ☐ Cheating
☐ Sexual harassment   ☐ Alcohol or drug possession

_____

_____

_____

_____

_____

Staff Signature: _____

Please contact the school office if you would like to discuss this form.

Source: Broad Acres Elementary. Reprinted with permission.

Figure 3.7: Sample of student referral form that includes student self-assessment of behavior.

Looking at data allows schools to evaluate the overall progress of their approach to behavior management. If the data show a significant reduction in office referrals, it makes sense to continue with the strategies that are in place; however, if there is only a modest change or no change at all (or an increase), the plan must be revised. The first and most important question to consider is whether or not staff is implementing the discipline plan with complete commitment and fidelity. This has less to do with finding fault or placing blame, and more to do with a staff being reflective about their work with students and problem solving as needed to make appropriate adjustments.

After looking at the global data to determine if office referrals for inappropriate behavior have decreased, leaders can analyze the data in a disaggregated fashion—looking at the data from several different vantage points. This is why collecting comprehensive data (typically a task assigned to one person) is critical. Breaking data down into referrals by grade, time of day, kind of behavior, location, race and culture, and gender allows leaders to look at each subcategory to see if there is one area that is a bigger problem than others. Do certain behaviors occur more often during specific times of the day, during specific months of the year, in certain areas of the school building, at specific grade levels, or with specific teachers?

An often difficult aspect of data analysis for decision making for principals is using the data they gather to provide feedback to and support for individual teachers. Geoff Colvin (2007) notes that:

> In some cases, it is clear that a majority of referrals, especially from classrooms, come from individual teachers. In these cases, the teacher may need additional assistance in addressing the problems. Careful attention must be given to how this information is communicated and addressed with the teacher, otherwise he or she could feel as though he or she is being singled out.

If leaders explain the data-collection process and set expectations before giving feedback, they can avoid many potential problems.

Using Data for Student Learning

The primary purpose of an effective schoolwide behavior and discipline plan is to create a safe, supportive, positive, and welcoming environment for all students and staff. Once this environment is established, educators are in a stronger position to provide effective instruction. It should be a goal to begin to see a connection between improved behavioral data and academic performance. Broad Acres Elementary found that over a five-year period, as their number of office referrals progressively decreased, their students' reading and math scores progressively increased (Broad Acres Elementary, personal communication, April 2012).

Summary

Managing problem behavior is part of the daily life of school personnel. Creating and maintaining an effective schoolwide behavior and discipline plan is key to creating a safe and secure learning environment for students. This plan should be developed by staff members as well as school leaders, such as by a leadership team, with all staff giving input into the final product. Positive behaviors need to be taught to students just as academic instruction is taught, and students need to receive regular rewards and reinforcement when they exhibit appropriate behaviors. When students exhibit poor behavior choices, they must have appropriate consequences. The office is responsible for managing specific problem behaviors, and by collecting data, schools can get feedback about whether or not their efforts are working. Collecting data, sharing data, analyzing data, and data-based decision making have to become a cultural and operational norm at the school.

Taking a Stand Against Bullying

*The message in schools and communities
must be crystal clear. No bullying allowed!*

—STAN KOKI

An important part of creating a physically and emotionally safe environment that is conducive to learning is taking a stand against bullying. Given the serious effects of bullying on students and schools, physical and verbal abuse can no longer be dismissed as an inevitable part of growing up. As the Northwest Regional Educational Laboratory (2001) has noted, "there is nothing normal about ongoing incidents of harassment, violence, and intimidation." In order to build safe and effective schools, it is essential to understand—and take seriously—the dynamics of bullying behavior among school-aged children.

What Is Bullying?

A student is being bullied or victimized when he or she is exposed, repeatedly and over time, to negative actions on the part of one or more other students. These negative actions can be verbal, nonverbal, or physical. Bullying has three key characteristics: (1) the bully intends to do harm, (2) the bullying occurs more than once, and (3) there is a power imbalance between the bully and victim (Bauman, 2008).

In the past, bullying was treated as an unfortunate though perhaps unavoidable part of growing up, but the problem has become pervasive and serious. Luckily, we know more than ever about the psychology of bullying. One study by researchers at York University and Queens University (Pepler, Jiang, Craig, & Connolly, 2008) sheds light on the psychology of bullying. The researchers tracked 871 students (466 girls and 405 boys) between the ages of ten and eighteen, interviewing them each year about their involvement in bullying or victimizing behavior, their relationships in general, and other positive and negative behaviors. They found the following:

- Most children said they engaged in bullying at some point during their school years.

- 9.9 percent said they engaged in consistently high levels of bullying from elementary through high schools.

- 35.1 percent said they bullied peers at moderate levels.

- 13.4 percent said they frequently bullied others in elementary school but engaged in very little bullying by the end of high school.

Given the widespread problem bullying has become, it is important to recognize its effects on the victims, bystanders, and on the bullies themselves. Students who are bullied often have difficulty concentrating on their schoolwork and may experience a decline in academic performance. Frequent taunting, teasing, or physical abuse may lead to feelings of anxiety. Victims of bullying experience higher than normal absenteeism and dropout rates and may exhibit more insecurity, anxiety, depression, loneliness, unhappiness, physical and mental symptoms, and low self-esteem than other students (Nansel et al., 2001, cited in Lumsden, 2002). When students are bullied on a regular basis, they may even become suicidal or homicidal.

Students who witness bullying also suffer from ill effects. Research conducted as part of the Maine Project Against Bullying (2000) suggests that simply being exposed to "violence and maltreatment (including verbal abuse) of others is significantly associated with increased depression, anxiety, anger, post-traumatic stress, alcohol use, and low grades."

The bullies themselves experience negative consequences arising from their aggressive behavior. Students who bully are often less popular when they get to high school, have few friends, and are more likely than other students to engage in criminal activity. As adults, students who bully have higher rates of substance abuse, domestic violence, and other violent crime (Ballard, Argus, & Remley, 1999).

Indeed, bullying has been linked to long-term effects—emotional damage, anxiety disorders, depression, addictions, and even schizophrenia and bipolar disorder—though the relationship between bullying and these types of problems is complex since bullies seem to zero in on children who seem "different" (Szalavitz, 2010). Bullying definitely has consequences, however, including on academic achievement. As psychiatrist Bruce Perry notes, "An educational climate that tolerates relational hostility and marginalization of children is doomed to be an academic as well as a social failure" (Szalavitz, 2010, p. C9).

The Challenges of Identifying and Combating Bullying

While all schools aim to be safe places for children, both physically and psychologically, many educators are less than effective at identifying and combating bullying. As one anonymous teacher said in a survey, "We are not addressing the whole problem. Children reflect the values and behavior they see in their homes, on television, and in video games." When children see adults, family members, even teachers and school administrators using bullying and intimidation tactics, some are likely to follow suit. In addition, many adults are ambivalent about bullying, regarding it as "not that bad." Some even believe that victims of bullying bring it on themselves and deserve what they get.

Reducing Bullying Behavior

The good news is that bullying behavior is more malleable than was commonly thought. According to Maia Szalavitz (2010), humans "are as well adapted to cooperate as to compete. The key is to create situations that enhance our kind side and play down the darker traits" (p. C9). This bringing out of the kind side is critically important for school administrators who set the school climate, which makes all the difference in establishing a school that is safe and tolerable, as opposed to one that is impossible to bear for students who are less socially adept and prone to bullying (Szalavitz, 2010). If school leaders tolerate bullying, then so will everyone else in the school community.

Looking the other way is clearly not an appropriate way to deal with the issue of bullying, but that leaves the question of what exactly leaders should do. A U.S. Department of Defense study found that one of the best ways to counteract the feeling of lack of social bonds experienced by many service members' children who move frequently from base to base is "school connectedness" (Szalavitz, 2010). Students in schools that are successful in creating a caring climate have fewer alcohol and drug problems, less early-age sexual activity, fewer suicidal thoughts and attempts, and better academic performance. By implementing a well-planned program of emphasizing kindness and mutual respect in both actions and words, school leaders can reduce bullying and create a physically and emotionally safe environment. Szalavitz (2010) notes that the most important element in such an endeavor "is system-wide determination—which starts from the top and permeates down—to support empathetic values. Staff must refuse to ignore acts of bullying and exclusion" (p. C9).

Rethinking Anti-Bullying Programs

Zero-tolerance, get-tough anti-bullying programs have received a lot of skepticism. These types of programs are dangerous because they make schools resemble prisons and increase the sense of danger and disrespect (Szalavitz, 2010). In addition, some worry that these programs have led to the creation of a huge, for-profit "bully prevention" industry that claims to be a panacea for schools' social ills (Brown, 2008). The danger here is that the prepackaged strategies with their rules, policies, consequences, and no-bullying posters can keep leaders and school staff from doing what they must do: listen well, think critically, and create approaches that meet the needs of their own schools and communities (Szalavitz, 2010).

Lyn Mikel Brown (2008) suggests the following alternative ideas to traditional bullying prevention programs:

- *Stop labeling kids.* Although critical to understanding the dynamics of bullying, publicly putting students into categories—bullies, victims, and bystanders—oversimplifies what happens in schools as everyone is capable of doing harm and good. In addition, labeling contributes to a negative culture and "downplays the important role of parents, teachers, and the school system, a provocative and powerful media culture, and societal injustices children experience every day" (p. 29). Labeling puts responsibility on the students alone without acknowledging these other factors.

- *Be specific about hurtful behavior.* It is important for educators to be specific about bullying behavior. This helps educate students about their rights, affirms their realities, encourages solutions, invites dialogue, allows students to be agents of social change, and helps to protect them.

- *Move beyond the individual.* Make an effort to understand why a student uses aggression towards other students. Many different factors affect a child's behavior—life history, social context, race, ethnicity, social class, gender, religion, and ability. These all have an impact on the student's experiences in school. Leaders and school staff should consider how these factors might affect the kinds of attention and resources the child receives, where he or she fits in, whether he or she feels marginalized or privileged, and so on.

- *Adjust your expectations.* Consider whether or not you are holding students accountable for ideals and expectations that adults could never meet. Is it fair to expect students to never express anger to adults or never to act in mean or hurtful ways to one another despite the fact that they may not feel safe and secure in school and feel as though they are disrespected by other students and even teachers? It is critical to promote consistent consequences for problem behavior, but it's also important to encourage students to think critically and question unfairness.

- *Listen to students.* Many bully-prevention programs are rife with rules, meetings, and trainings from adults. Take time to listen to students to try and understand their world and experiences. Include them in the discussion about school norms and rules.

- *Accentuate the positive.* Anti-bullying efforts should identify students as potential leaders and affirm student strengths. They should place hope in student behavior. These efforts should not be about controlling students; rather, anti-bullying strategies should give students more personal control.

Implementing Anti-Bullying Strategies

Educators Donna San Antonio and Elizabeth Salzfass (2007) report that the biggest worries among students entering middle schools are not having any friends and being made fun of. In a survey of students in a big city, small city, and rural middle school, the authors found widespread bullying, particularly of students seen as being overweight, poorly dressed, gay, "different," or "weird." Students said they could not count on adults to prevent bullying and intervene when it occurred. San Antonio and Salzfass believe that adults hold the keys to creating a safe and accepting climate for all students. They suggest the following steps:

1. *Conduct an assessment.* Find out where, when, and how bullying is taking place so that anti-bullying efforts can be targeted to the school's particular circumstances.

2. *Create a committee on in-school social dynamics.* The committee should include staff, students, parents, and community members and look at student social dynamics.

3. *Implement an anti-bullying policy.* This policy should include a definition of bullying, a schoolwide commitment to address the issue, a statement of everyone's rights and responsibilities as they relate to bullying, the ways students and staff will identify and respond to bullying, how the administration will respond, and a way to measure how well anti-bullying efforts are working.

4. *Recognize and name all types of bullying.* Types of bullying can range from blatant comments about racial, ethnic, or social groups to below-the-radar whispering, rumor spreading, and exclusion.

5. *Train all school employees.* Everyone, including custodians, clerical and cafeteria staff, and bus drivers, should know how to spot bullying and follow up.

6. *Help students who are bullied.* Victims of bullying need to be heard either in one-on-one or group sessions. This is particularly important for students who have experienced unfairness or violence at home.

7. *Work with bullies.* Once identified, perpetrators need consequences and counseling. One effective approach is pair counseling, in which two students who are having difficulty with peer relationships meet with a counselor to negotiate differences and learn how to be a friend.

8. *Name and reclaim goodness.* An often overlooked but essential aspect of creating emotionally and socially safe environments is noticing and acknowledging acts of kindness, which can be risky for students and could put their own social standing in jeopardy.

San Antonio and Salzfass (2007) suggest that social-emotional education should be integrated into the academic curriculum in the following ways:

- It should become part of a school and community discussion about values, beliefs about how to treat one another, and policies that reflect these values—specifically how adults in the school will respond when bullying occurs.

- It should pose developmentally and culturally appropriate social dilemmas for discussion and address all types of bullying.

- It should teach students how to resolve tensions and disagreements nonviolently and without losing face.

- It should challenge the idea that aggression and bullying are inevitable and expected behaviors among students and the idea that the victim's behavior causes bullying.

- It should foster critical thinking by students and reject stereotypes about bullying, such as the idea that boys use physical aggression and girls use relational aggression.

- It should help children look critically at popular culture and link in-school bullying to broader issues of social injustice.

- It should encourage students to speak up about bullying and help them generate realistic and credible ways to stay safe.

Dealing With Cyberbullying

The Internet has become a prime place for bullying. It provides more opportunities for students to bully and to be bullied, and because online interactions are not face-to-face or can be anonymous, they appear to lessen the bully's accountability. Students themselves attest to this. As one student said, "It's easier to fight online because you feel more brave and in control. On Facebook, you can be as mean as you want" (Hoffman, 2010).

In addition to diminished accountability for students who bully, there is a lot of confusion over exactly who is responsible for protecting students. Cyberbullying most often happens outside of school, after school hours. However, the effects of this bullying make their way into the school. For example, Jan Hoffman (2010) reports that:

> Many parents are looking to schools for justice, protection, even revenge. . . .
> But many educators feel unprepared or unwilling to be prosecutors and judges
> . . . Reluctant to assert an authority they are not sure they have, educators can
> appear indifferent to parents frantic with worry, alarmed by recent adolescent
> suicides linked to bullying.

Establishing accountability for such online bullying is problematic; there has been no clear guidance from the justice system. Given that the laws regarding cyberbullying are still developing, it's not surprising that principals vary greatly in their responses to it. Some suspend students who torment their peers online while others say that their hands are tied when students bully others outside of school hours. Some researchers, such as Bernard James, believe administrators are interpreting the law too narrowly. "Educators are empowered to maintain safe schools," he says. "The timidity of educators in this context of emerging technology is working to the advantage of bullies" (Hoffman, 2010). Essentially, his message is that while the issues of both student and adult accountability are far from clear, educators cannot afford to ignore them.

So what can school leaders do to prevent this kind of bullying? Nancy Willard (2006) says that adults need to become more involved in the online lives of students and make it clear that they will respond (and help) when someone crosses the line. Many students do not report incidents of cyberbullying because they assume that school leaders can or will do nothing to stop it or because they are (sometimes rightly) afraid that their own access to the Internet will be restricted. However, when students realize that adults can and will respond effectively, they are more likely to report bullying.

Becoming aware of incidents of cyberbullying is an excellent first step for school administrators. Willard (2006) recommends that if cyberbullying is reported, schools should respond by conducting individualized searches of the Internet activities of those students through the district's Internet system. This proactive stance by schools is crucial, says Willard, "If students are engaging in cyberbullying at school and the school is not engaged in reasonable efforts to detect, prevent, and respond to it, the potential for liability is real" (p. 43).

Types of Cyberbullying

- Flaming: Online fights using angry, vulgar electronic messages.
- Harassment: Repeatedly sending offensive, rude, and insulting messages.
- Denigration: "Dissing" someone online with insulting, denigrating gossip or rumors.
- Impersonation: Getting a person's password and posing as him or her online.
- Outing and trickery: Sharing someone's secrets or embarrassing information online.
- Exclusion: Intentionally keeping someone out of an online group (for example, a buddy list).
- Cyberstalking: Repeatedly sending unwanted messages that may include threats.

Source: Willard (2006).

But what if cyberbullying is happening outside school hours and doesn't involve the school's Internet system? The legal standard for taking disciplinary action, says Willard (2006), is that the bullying must create a "substantial and material disruption or threat of disruption at school" for school administration to take action. If off-campus bullying is discovered or suspected, principals should contact parents and urge them to install monitoring software on their home computers.

School and home monitoring of students' online activities goes a long way toward re-establishing both student and parent accountability in online bullying. But school leaders can also take a more traditional route for dealing with the problem. If students feel comfortable reporting incidents of cyberbullying, school leaders can respond by simply gathering the students in question and starting a face-to-face conversation.

Finally, school leaders need to initiate and continue their own frank dialogues about the issue of accountability and how far adults can go to stop cyberbullying. Principals should consider such questions as, can leaders search a computer or a cell phone the way they search a locker or a backpack, and what should a school's code of discipline say about cyber communication? Conversations among leaders are likely to lead to schoolwide policies that can then be communicated to parents and community members.

Enlisting the School Counselor

The school guidance counselor is in a unique position to play a significant role in counseling and providing support for students who bully and are the victims of bullies. There must be a point person if anti-bullying efforts are to get traction, and Sheri Bauman (2008) believes that the person ideally situated to play this role, at least in elementary schools, is the counselor:

> Contemporary school counselors already are school leaders, consultants to other staff and to the larger community, classroom educators, parent educators, and individual and group counselors. They can collect and use data and are instrumental in establishing and maintaining a positive school climate. They are consensus builders and facilitators of task groups. Who better to assume responsibility and leadership in bullying reduction? (p. 369)

Counselors, if given clear responsibility by the principal, can play a number of roles (Bauman, 2008): providing colleagues with a clear definition of bullying and its various forms (physical, verbal, and relational); making the case for eliminating bullying; doing staff training to address all-too-common "rite of passage" attitudes; educating staff on the signs of bullying and the most effective interventions; alerting staff to ineffective ways of dealing with bullying (especially peer mediation, which doesn't work because of the power imbalance in bullying situations); monitoring supervision of unstructured times, when bullying is most likely to occur; tracking data to see when and where bullying is occurring and what's working and what isn't; and, of course, providing one-on-one and small-group counseling to students involved in bullying.

In addition, Ballard, Argus, and Remley (1999) offer the following suggestions for counselors:

- Provide an anonymous way for students to request to see the counselor or report bullying, such as a locked suggestion box. This strategy provides students with a safe way to report bullying since they are often reluctant to do so.

- When the bullying of a student by another student has been reported, speak with each student individually. This allows counselors to understand both students' perspectives, which allows them to determine specific intervention strategies.

In addition to helping the victim deal with his or her victimization, Walter B. Roberts, Jr. and Diane H. Coursol (1996), suggest that a counselor consider what the student's life is like from a broader perspective and if there are resources and support systems available for the student in the home. By giving thought to questions such as these, a counselor can evaluate the likelihood of a repeat victimization experience and the child's likely reaction to ongoing bullying episodes. Children who are frequently bullied may resort to violence themselves; it is this type of reaction that counselors, teachers, and administrators need to prevent by monitoring and intervening when necessary.

Educating Parents

Like many teachers, many parents also view bullying as a rite of passage and do not take their child's concerns seriously, if the child relays them to the parent at all. Many parents also do not understand the negative effect bullying can have on academic performance. Given this, principals need to take the initiative to inform parents about the seriousness of bullying and the detrimental effect it can have on their child's self-esteem and academic performance.

In an effort to curb bullying through parent awareness, some schools have initiated programs directed at the parents of students who physically or verbally abuse other students. For example, an elementary school in California requires parents of students at risk for expulsion to attend regular meetings to discuss possible solutions to their child's behavior problems. Parent-management training is another option. This intervention strategy teaches parents effective methods of behavior management to decrease their child's aggressive behavior (Peterson & Skiba, 2001).

According to the Northwest Regional Educational Laboratory (2001), the most critical thing for adults to do is listen. Some parent programs may focus on this skill of listening by teaching parents to communicate better with their children. The objective of such programs is often encouraging parents to take time to talk with their children—to find out what is going on in their lives, how they feel about themselves, and their overall well-being. Children who feel they can openly talk to their parents are more likely to report incidences of bullying to them than children who do not have good relationships with the adults in their lives.

Summary

Bullying is all too common in schools today. School leaders must help their staff and community realize that it is not acceptable and not just part of growing up. They must help stakeholders and students develop a common definition of bullying. Schools must implement strategies to address bullying behaviors, including cyberbullying, and call on school counselors and parents to support the schoolwide initiative.

5

Addressing Issues of Safety and Security

If education is important to us, then a safe learning environment must occur in all of our schools so that children feel safe, comfortable, and prepared to learn.

—J. ARGON

While serious incidents of crime and violence in schools are rare, the possibility that they could occur cannot be ignored. Events of the late 1990s and 2000s have demonstrated that these crimes do not discriminate; schools in suburban and rural areas are just as likely to fall victim to violent acts as those in large, urban areas. The principal has a key leadership role in creating and maintaining a safe learning environment for students and staff. School leaders must plan for the worst and take a proactive approach to dealing with the possibility of violence or other crises at their schools.

Much of what has been discussed in the previous chapters can be viewed as ways to guard against violent acts by members of the school community. Students who view the school as a caring place for learning are simply much less likely to engage in inappropriate and violent behavior. Kevin Dwyer, David Osher, and Cynthia Warger (1998) recommend that by understanding what leads to violence and how school leaders and teachers can prevent violence effectively, leaders can make their schools safer. If everyone in the school community—administrators, teachers, families, students, support staff, and community members—identify warning signs early, students can get the help they need to prevent violence from occurring.

But building a caring learning community and attempting to address the needs of all students is not enough. In addition, safe schools carefully develop comprehensive procedures for safety-related issues. In these schools, staff and students are educated about these procedures and provided with training so that in a crisis, they follow key steps and exhibit key behaviors. Finally, in safe schools, there is an explicit effort to ensure that everyone is kept informed about problems that have occurred or might occur.

Creating a Physically Safe Environment

A safe physical environment promotes a sense of security and comfort to students and staff alike. Students who feel safe in their surroundings often display a more positive attitude towards learning. Principals can enhance physical safety by doing the following (Dwyer, Osher, & Warger, 1998):

- Supervising access to buildings and grounds

- Adjusting scheduling to minimize time in hallways or in potentially dangerous locations

- Having adults visibly present throughout the school building

- Staggering dismissal times and lunch periods

- Coordinating with local police to ensure there are safe routes to and from school

Ronald D. Stephens (1998) suggests school leaders establish crisis-management policies that involve school staff, students, parents, law enforcement officials, community emergency services, and the media, in addition to providing staff with training. School leaders can conduct annual school-safety site assessments. These assessments will help identify facilities that are poorly managed and maintained, which are a liability. Landscaping and architecture that restrict natural supervision should be adjusted, and broken windows and malfunctioning doors should be repaired. In addition, leaders should share information among schools and staff members about dangerous conditions or people. Stephens points out that there's a trend toward requiring school officials to be notified of dangerous people in and near schools. This also includes notifying school officials when students with violent or criminal backgrounds are transferred into or within a school district.

Many student conflicts occur in undefined public spaces in and around school buildings—in places that teachers and other adults do not frequent or supervise and where students feel they have little ownership. Hallways, parking lots, stairwells, and cafeterias are among the most common "unowned places" for conflict (Astor, Meyer, & Behre, 1999). Metal detectors and surveillance cameras are largely ineffective in preventing conflicts or violence in these areas; students believe that the unowned places must be personally secured by competent, trusted adults. Educators should take social patterns (like crowded cafeterias and hallways) and building characteristics (like remote stairwells and large parking lots) into consideration when planning an environment that promotes caring and discourages violence. Despite this, security devices and other safety measures have become commonplace in many schools. John E. Kosar and Ahmed Faruq (2000) view the use of closed-circuit television cameras to monitor public corridors, parking lots, playgrounds, stairwells, gymnasiums, and cafeterias as a cost-effective safety measure.

Planning for a Crisis

By now, just about every school has developed a crisis plan, covering procedures for incidents as varied as severe weather, evacuations, hazardous material accidents, lockdowns, bomb threats, and death and suicides. Terrence Quinn (2002) describes an effective crisis-prevention and response plan as one that:

> Spells out how all members of the school community—administrators, teachers, support staff, parents, and students—will be trained to identify symptoms of a potential crisis. The prevention plan should describe school and community resources and how these resources can be utilized to maintain a safe environment. It should also describe effective prevention strategies and intervention approaches.

He adds that training should be conducted annually for teachers and staff. Sessions should address a plan overview, counseling techniques, and a complete review of procedures. Million (2002) points out that many schools have failed to hold their crisis plans up to thorough testing. A safe school does not consider planning finished until the necessary procedures are practiced and the rough spots smoothed out.

Key Ingredients of a Crisis Plan

A comprehensive crisis plan should include the following:

- A list of crisis team members and their roles
- A telephone tree of staff phone numbers to call in emergencies
- A list of essential emergency numbers (police, fire, hospital, and so on)
- A list of personnel with special expertise (such as CPR and first aid)
- Emergency procedures (in case of intruders, bomb threats, and so on)
- A special code to alert team members
- Staff schedules
- A school map showing locations of bathrooms, phones, and exits
- Sample letters (crisis announcements, condolences, and so on)
- The location of the school emergency supply kit, which should include a battery-powered bullhorn, first-aid kit, and a list of students with medical needs
- An evaluation method to assess the plan's effectiveness

Source: Quinn (2002).

Developing a Crisis Team

For a crisis plan to succeed, a well-informed and capable crisis team needs to be in place. Members of this team develop the plan and coordinate activities during an actual crisis. The team should include the principal and other school administrators, security personnel, custodians, school nurse, mental health specialists (such as a guidance counselor, school psychologist, or social worker), and several teachers. Quinn (2002) suggests some specific elements for this task:

1. *Assign specific roles to each team member.* Essential roles include security coordinator, staff liaison, student contact liaison, internal communications liaison, external communications liaison, parent liaison, team recorder, and crisis observer.

2. *Delineate the responsibilities of each team member.* The following are examples of this:

   › The *security coordinator* must secure the building, supervise entry and departure, and maintain emergency communication equipment (cell phones, walkie-talkies).

   › The *staff liaison* must organize a system for staff members to communicate their concerns to the crisis team, assess staff reaction to a crisis, and provide necessary support.

   › The *student contact liaison* is responsible for providing emotional support for students, particularly those with special needs.

   › The *internal communications liaison* is assigned to share information with staff and students and make available space and materials for crisis team meetings. This person must have access to the school's telephones, cell phones, and computers and may be assisted by staff or student couriers trained to deliver messages quickly and accurately.

   › The *external communications liaison* supervises dedicated phone lines, manages incoming and outgoing information, logs all calls, screens messages, and provides prepared statements in the event of phone inquiries related to a crisis.

   › The *parent liaison* sets up a parent support center, organizes the release of students to parents during a crisis, and informs parents about available counseling services for their children.

   › The *crisis observer* provides feedback about individual and group behaviors during a crisis and keeps the team focused on issues to be addressed.

   › The *team recorder* keeps all records of the crisis, maintains a list of all team decisions, and uses this information to prepare a final after-crisis report.

Developing a Crisis Procedure Checklist

During a crisis, a sense of routine—with everyone having an almost automatic sense of what he or she should be doing and when—is critical. Use the following list (Dwyer et al., 1998, p. 29) to review what procedures your school already has in place and what procedures need to be addressed. After a crisis, identify trouble spots and revise your procedures to deal more effectively with those challenges. The following are examples of this:

• Assess life and safety issues immediately.

- Provide immediate emergency medical care.

- Call 911 and notify police and rescue personnel first. Call the superintendent second.

- Convene the crisis team to assess the situation and implement the crisis response procedures.

- Evaluate available and needed resources.

- Alert school staff to the situation.

- Activate the crisis communication procedure and system of verification.

- Secure all areas.

- Implement evacuation and other procedures to protect students and staff from harm.

- Avoid dismissing students to unknown care.

- Adjust the bell schedule to ensure safety during a crisis.

- Alert persons in charge of various information systems to prevent confusion and misinformation.

- Contact appropriate community agencies and the school district's public information office if appropriate.

Stress Safety and Preparedness

Parents must know that the school is as prepared as it can be. So every chance they get—at back-to-school nights, PTA meetings, in newsletters, during conversations, in the school's handbook and on the school's website—principals should stress safety and preparedness. This helps build confidence (Million, 2002).

Summary

While no principal—and no school—can prepare for every crisis or emergency, comprehensive, well-thought-out procedures and a well-trained staff and student body are critical to the development of a caring learning community. At best, it may help to keep the school and students more secure, and if a crisis or dangerous situation does occur, planning can minimize the harm to students and staff.

AFTERWORD

Concluding Thoughts for School Leaders

[It would be a] mistake to consider the creation of a safe and supportive school community as an add-on effort. . . . Unless the school has a clear sense of its vision and goals, along with a comprehensive plan to realize them, such programs will likely do little to positively affect the daily experiences of most students and staff.

—LEARNING FIRST ALLIANCE

The purpose of this book is to provide school leaders with clear steps for creating physical and emotional safety in their schools—to build a strong foundation for student learning. If schools are not physically and emotionally safe for students, students will be less available for learning and teachers will be forced to spend a great deal of time and energy dealing with persistent discipline problems, resulting in less time for instruction. When students and adults alike have peace of mind about school and predictability with regard to expectations, they can flourish.

Whether your school has serious discipline problems or is already a safe and emotionally supportive school that simply wants to get better, the starting point for your work should be developing a vision of what the school community would like to become. As principal, pulling together the often-complex pieces of a physically secure and emotionally supportive environment is one of your most important responsibilities. As with so many other aspects of school improvement, it requires planning, collaboration among staff, efforts to educate students and staff about problems and possible solutions, attention to detail, and ongoing evaluation to identify what does and does not work.

The strategies and steps presented in this book take considerable effort and commitment from faculty and administration. Moreover, developing a caring learning community with a schoolwide behavior and discipline plan is not a once-and-done task. Rather, it will involve revisiting, assessment, refinement, and maintenance. The importance of the principal's role in this process cannot be overstated. As with almost any school initiative, the only way for consistent and widespread implementation is with the engaged support of the principal. The principal provides lighthouse leadership to help staff and students learn together, implement that learning, and be accountable. Without the principal taking an active role in shepherding the initiative, a school will—at best— have only pockets of excellence. Through your leadership and hard work in this process, you have tremendous power to influence what the school experience will be for your students, and students who feel safe and emotionally supported are more able to focus on learning.

REFERENCES AND RESOURCES

American Psychological Association. (1996). *Is youth violence just another fact of life? Some kids resilient; Some kids at risk*. Washington, DC: Author.

Astor, R. A., Meyer, H. A., & Behre, W. J. (1999). Unowned places and times: Maps and interviews about violence in high schools. *American Educational Research Journal, 36*(1), 3–42.

Author, A. A. (2009). Bulletin board: Resources on cyberbullying. *Principal Leadership, 9*(6), 10.

Ballard, M., Argus, T., & Remley, T. P., Jr. (1999). Bullying and school violence: A proposed prevention program. *NASSP Bulletin, 83*(607), 38–47.

Barth, R. S. (2006). Improving relationships within the schoolhouse. *Improving Professional Practice, 63*(6), 8–13.

Bauman, S. (2008). The role of elementary school counselors in reducing school bullying. *Elementary School Journal, 108*(5), 362–375.

Bear, G., Doyle, W., Ocher, D., & Sprague, J. (2010). How can we improve school discipline? *Educational Researcher, 39*(1), 48–58.

Bennis, W. (1997). The secrets of great groups. *Leader to Leader, 3*, 29–33.

Bodine, R. J., & Crawford, D. K. (1998). *The handbook of conflict resolution education: A guide to building quality programs in schools*. San Francisco: Jossey-Bass.

Bogen, M. (2009). Beyond the discipline handbook—A conversation with George Sugai. *Harvard Education Letter, 25*(3), 8, 6.

Borelli, J. (2007). A discipline plan that works. *Principal, 87*(1), 38.

Boyer, E. L. (1995). *The basic school: A community for learning*. Princeton, NJ: The Carnegie Foundation for the Advancement of Teaching.

Brookes, R. (n.d.). *Education and "charismatic" adults: To touch a student's heart and mind*. Accessed at www.drrobertbrooks.com/writings/articles/0009.html on December 27, 2011.

Brown, L. M. (2008). 10 ways to move beyond bully prevention (And why we should). *Education Week, 27*(26), 29.

Brownell, M. T., & Walther-Thomas, C. (1999). An interview with Dr. Michael Rosenberg: Preventing school discipline problems schoolwide. *Intervention in School and Clinic, 35*(2), 108–112.

Buffum, A., Mattos, M., & Weber, C. (2008). *Pyramid response to intervention: RTI, professional learning communities, and how to respond when kids don't learn*. Bloomington, IN: Solution Tree Press.

Buffum, A., Mattos, M., & Weber, C. (2012). *Simplifying response to intervention: Four essential guiding principles*. Bloomington, IN: Solution Tree Press.

Canter, L. (2006). *Classroom management for academic success*. Bloomington, IN: Solution Tree Press.

Center on Positive Behavioral Interventions and Supports. (2004). *School-wide positive behavior support: Implementers' blueprint and self-assessment*. Washington, DC: U.S. Department of Education.

Clarke, S. H., & Campbell, F. A. (1998). Can intervention early prevent crime later? The abecedarian project compared with other programs. *Early Childhood Research Quarterly, 13*(2), 319–343.

Cohen, J. (Ed.). (2001). *Caring classrooms/intelligent schools: The social emotional education of young children*. New York: Teachers College Press.

Coleman, C., Hierck, T., & Weber, C. (2011). *Pyramid of behavior intervention: 7 keys to a positive learning environment*. Bloomington, IN: Solution Tree Press.

Colvin, G. (2007). *7 Steps for developing discipline: A guide for principals and leadership teams*. Thousand Oaks, CA: Corwin Press.

Conzemius, A. E., & Morganti-Fisher, T. (2012). *More than a SMART goal: Staying focused on student learning*. Bloomington, IN: Solution Tree Press.

Cotton, K. (1995). *If effective schools research summary; 1995 update*. Portland, OR: North West Regional Educational Laboratory.

Cotton, K. (2001). *Schoolwide and classroom discipline* (School Improvement Research Series Close-Up #9). Accessed at http://educationnorthwest.org/webfm_send/530 on February 8, 2012.

Cross, N. (2008). The power of expectations. *Principal Leadership, 9*(3), 24–28.

Davis, C., & Yang, A. (2009). Keeping in touch with families all year long. *Responsive Education Digest, 75*(1), 61–64.

DuFour, R., DuFour, R., Eaker, R., & Many, T. (2010). *Learning by doing: A handbook for professional learning communities at work* (2nd ed.). Bloomington, IN: Solution Tree Press.

Dunsworth, M., & Billings, D. (2009). *The high-performing school: Benchmarking the 10 indicators of effectiveness*. Bloomington, IN: Solution Tree Press.

Durlak, J. A., Weissberg, R. P., Dymnicki, A. B., & Schellinger, K. B. (2011). The impact of enhancing students' social and emotional learning: A meta-analysis of school-based universal interventions. *Child Development, 82*(1), 405–432.

Dweck, C. (2007). *Mindset: The new psychology of success*. New York: Ballantine Books.

Dwyer, K. & Osher, D. (2000). *Safeguarding our children: An action guide: Implementing early warning, timely response*. Washington, DC: U.S. Department of Education. Accessed at www2.ed.gov/admins/lead/safety/actguide/action_guide.pdf on December 27, 2011.

Dwyer, K., Osher, D., & Warger, C. (1998). *Early warning, timely response: A guide to safe schools*. Washington, DC: U.S. Department of Education. Accessed at http://cecp.air.org/guide/guide.pdf on December 27, 2011.

Educational Research Service. (1997). *Principal's survival kit*. Arlington, VA: Author.

Federman, J. (Ed.). (1998). *National television violence study*: Executive summary (Vol. 3). Santa Barbara: University of California, Santa Barbara.

Franek, M. (2006). Foiling cyberbullies in the new wild west. *Educational Leadership, 63*(4), 39–43.

Fullan, M. (2003). *The moral imperative of school leadership*. Thousand Oaks, CA: Corwin Press.

George, M. P., & White, G. P. (n.d.). *Implementing school-wide behavior change: Lessons from the field.* Bethlehem, PA: Lehigh University.

George, M. P., White, G. P., & Schlaffer, J. J. (2007). Implementing school-wide behavior change: Lessons from the field. *Psychology in the Schools, 41*(1), 41–51.

Goleman, G. (2002). Leading resonant teams. *Leader to Leader, 25.*

Guetzloe, E., & Rockwell, S. (1998). Fight, flight, or better choices: Teaching nonviolent responses to young children. *Preventing School Failure, 42*(4), 154–159.

Hartzell, G. N., & Petrie, T. A. (1992). The principal and discipline: Working with school structures, teachers, and students. *The Clearing House, 65*(6), 376–380.

Heflebower, T. (2011, July 18). The ten- and two-minute intervention. Presented at a professional development seminar for *The highly engaged classroom* in Raytown, MO.

Hoffman, J. (2010, June 27). Online bullies pull schools into the fray. *New York Times Magazine.* Accessed at www .nytimes.com/2010/06/28/style/28bully.html?pagewanted=1&_r=2&ref=general&src=me on April 1, 2012.

Horner, R. H., Sugai, G., & Horner, H. F. (2000). A schoolwide approach to student discipline. *The School Administrator, 57*(2), 20–23.

Horner, R. H., Sugai, G., Todd, A. W., & Lewis-Palmer, T. (2005). School-wide positive behavior support: An alternative approach to discipline in schools. In. L. Bambara & L. Kern (Eds.), *Positive behavior support* (pp. 359–390). New York: Guilford.

Horton, A. (1996). Teaching anger management skills to primary-age children. *Teaching and Change, 3*(3), 281–296.

Independent School District of Boise City. (2001). *Guidance & counseling programs K–12: Elementary counseling.* Accessed at www.boiseschools.org/counselors/elem.html on December 27, 2011.

Jeynes, W. (2010). The salience of the subtle aspects of parental involvement and encouraging that involvement: Implications for school-based programs. *Teachers College Record, 112*(3), 747–774.

Johnson, D. W., & Johnson, R. T. (1995a). *Reducing school violence through conflict resolution.* Alexandria, VA: Association for Supervision and Curriculum Development.

Johnson, D. W., & Johnson, R. T. (1995b). Why violence prevention programs don't work—And what does. *Educational Leadership, 52*(5), 63–67.

Johnson, D. W., Johnson, R. T., Dudley, B., & Burnett, R. (1992). Teaching students to be peer mediators. *Educational Leadership, 50*(1), 10–13.

Kanter, R. M. (2006). *Confidence: How winning and losing streaks begin and end.* New York: Crown Business.

Katz, N., & Lawyer, J. (1993). *Conflict resolution.* Thousand Oaks, CA: Corwin Press.

Koki, S. (1999). *Bullying in schools should not be par for the course.* Honolulu, HI: Pacific Resources for Education and Learning.

Kosar, J. E., & Faruq, A. (2000). Building security into schools. *The School Administrator, 57*(2), 24–26.

Kouzes, J. M., & Posner, B. Z. (1999). *Encouraging the heart: A leader's guide to rewarding and recognizing others* (1st ed.). San Franisco: Jossey-Bass.

Kouzes, J., & Posner, B. (2008). *The leadership challenge* (4th ed.). San Francisco: Jossey-Bass.

Kreidler, W. J. (1996). When anger rears its ugly head: How to teach students to cool off. *Instructor, 105*(7), 24–25.

Kuranz, M. (2002). Cultivating student potential. *Professional School Counseling, 5*(3), 172–179.

Labi, N. (2001, March 25). Let bullies beware. *Time.* Accessed at www.time.com/time/nation/article/0,8599,103822-1,00.html on December 27, 2011.

Larson, J. (2008). Angry and aggressive students. *Principal Leadership,* 12–15. Accessed at www.nasponline.org/resources/principals/Angry%20and%20Aggressive%20Students-NASSP%20Jan%2008.pdf on January 5, 2012.

Learning First Alliance. (2001). *Every child learning: Safe and supportive schools.* Baltimore: Author.

Lickona, T. (1991). *Educating for character: How our schools can teach respect and responsibility.* New York: Bantam Books.

Lumsden, L. (2002). *Preventing bullying* (ERIC digest). Washington, DC: ERIC Clearinghouse on Educational Management. Accessed at http://ericcass.uncg.edu/virtuallib/bullying/1068.html.

Lupton-Smith, H., Caruthers, W., et al. (1996). Conflict resolution as peer mediation: Programs for elementary, middle, and high school students. *The School Counselor, 43*(5), 374–391.

Maine Project Against Bullying. (2000). *A survey of bullying behavior among Maine third graders.* Accessed at http://lincoln.midcoast.com/~wps/against/bullying.html on December 27, 2011.

Marriott, D. (2001). Managing school culture. *Principal, 81*(1), 75–77.

Marzano, R. (2003). *Classroom management that works.* Alexandria, VA: Association for Supervision and Curriculum Development.

Marzano, R., Pickering, D., & Heflebower, T. (2011). *The highly engaged classroom.* Bloomington, IN: Marzano Research Laboratory.

MetLife. (2010). *The MetLife survey of the American teacher: Collaborating for student success.* Accessed at www.eric.ed.gov/PDFS/ED509650.pdf on December 28, 2011.

Michigan Department of Education. (2010). *School-wide positive behavioral interventions & supports: Implementation guide.* Lansing, MI: Center for Educational Networking.

Miles, B. H. (1999). Getting everybody on the same page: Conducting a behavior audit. *The High School Magazine, 6(7),* 30–32.

Million, J. (2002). Expecting the worst may be what's best. *NAESP Principal Online: PR Primer.* Accessed at www.naesp.org/comm/pr0302.htm.

Muhammad, A. (2009). *Transforming school culture: How to overcome staff division.* Bloomington, IN: Solution Tree Press.

Moles, O. C. (Ed.). (1996). *Reaching all families: Creating family-friendly schools.* Washington, DC: U.S. Department of Education.

National Resource Center for Safe Schools. (1999). *Recognizing and preventing bullying* (Fact sheet). Portland, OR: Author.

Northwest Regional Educational Laboratory. (2001). *By request . . . Schoolwide prevention of bullying.* Portland, OR: Northwest Regional Educational Laboratory. Accessed at http://educationnorthwest.org/webfm_send/465 on February 8, 2012.

Olweus, D. (1993). *Bullying at school: What we know and what we can do.* Cambridge, MA: Blackwell.

Payne, M., Conroy, S., & Racine, L. (1998). Creating positive school climates: This we believe and now we must act. *Middle School Journal, 30*(2), 65–67.

Pepler, D., Jiang, D., Craig, W., & Connolly, J. (2008). Developmental trajectories of bullying and associated factors. *Child Development,* 79, 325–338.

Peterson, R. L., & Skiba, R. (2001). Creating school climates that prevent school violence. *The Clearing House, 74*(3), 155–163.

Petrilli, M. (2008, July 17). The genius of American education. *The Education Gadfly, 8*(27), 2–4.

Posner, M. (1994). Research raises troubling questions about violence prevention programs. *Harvard Education Letter, 10*(3), 1–4.

Power, F. C., & Makogon, T. A. (1996). The just-community approach to care. *Journal for a Just and Caring Education, 2*(1), 9–24.

Protheroe, N. (2005). A schoolwide approach to discipline: Firmness, fairness, and consistency are the keys to an effective discipline program. *Principal, 84*(5), 41–44. Accessed at www.naesp.org/resources/2/ Principal/2005/M-Jp41.pdf on December 28, 2011.

Putnam, L. (1997). Productive conflict: Negotiation as implicit coordination. In C. DeDreu & E. Van de Vliert (Eds.), *Using conflict in organizations* (pp. 9–22). London: SAGE.

Quinlan, A. (2004). Six steps to successful conflict mediation. *Principal Magazine, 82*(4), 69.

Quinn, T. (2002). The inevitable school crisis: Are you ready? *Principal Magazine, 81*(5), 6–8.

Remboldt, C. (1998). Making violence unacceptable. *Educational Leadership, 56*(1), 32–38.

Roberts, W. B., Jr., & Coursol, D. H. (1996). Strategies for intervention with childhood and adolescent victims of bullying, teasing, and intimidation in school settings. *Elementary School Guidance and Counseling, 30*(3), 204–212.

Robinson, T. R., Smith, S. W., & Daunic, A. P. (2000). Middle school students' views on the social validity of peer mediation. *Middle School Journal, 31*(5), 23–29.

Sabatino, D. A. (1997). Replacing anger with trust. *Reclaiming Children and Youth, 6*(3), 167–170.

San Antonio, D., & Salzfass, E. (2007). How we treat one another in school. *Educational Leadership, 64*(8), 32–38. Accessed at www.ascd.org/publications/educational-leadership/may07/vol64/num08/How-We-Treat-One -Another-in-School.aspx on April 27, 2012.

ScienceDaily. (2008, March 25). Children who bully also have problems with other relationships. Accessed at www. sciencedaily.com/releases/2008/03/080325083300.htm on December 28, 2011.

Segal, J. (1988). Teachers have enormous power in affecting a child's self-esteem. *Brown University Child Behavior and Development Newsletter, 4,* 1–3.

Sprague, J. (2007). *Creating schoolwide prevention and intervention strategies.* Eugene: Institute on Violence and Destructive Behavior, University of Oregon.

Stephens, R. D. (1998). Ten steps to safer schools. *The American School Board Journal, 185*(3), 30–33.

Stockard, J., & Mayberry, M. (1992). *Effective educational environments.* Newbury Park, CA: Corwin Press.

Stolp, S. (1995). Every school a community: The academic value of strong social bonds among staff and students. *Oregon School Study Council Bulletin, 39*(1), 2–53.

Stone, C. B., & Clark, M. A. (2001). School counselors and principals: Partners in support of academic achievement. *NASSP Bulletin, 85*(624), 46–53.

Studer, J. (1996). Understanding and preventing aggressive responses in youth. *Elementary School Guidance and Counseling, 30*(3), 194–203.

Szalavitz, M. (2010, April 4). School empathy first line against bullies. *The Boston Globe*, p. C9.

Todd, A. W., Horner, R. H., & Tobin, T. J. (2007). *SWIS documentation project: Referral form definitions (version 4.1)*. Eugene: University of Oregon. Accessed at www.pbis.org/common/cms/documents/NewTeam/Data/ReferralFormDefinitions.pdf on April 27, 2012

U.S. Department of Education. (1998). *Preventing bullying: A manual for schools and communities*. Washington, DC: Author. Accessed at www.eric.ed.gov/PDFS/ED453592.pdf m on February 8, 2012.

U.S. Secret Service & U.S. Department of Education. (2002a). *The final report and findings of the Safe School Initiative: Implications for the prevention of school attacks in the United States*. Washington, DC: Authors.

U.S. Secret Service & U.S. Department of Education. (2002b). *Threat assessment in schools: A guide to managing threatening situations and to creating safe school climates*. Washington, DC: Authors. Accessed at www.secretservice.gov/ntac/ssi_guide.pdf on January 5, 2012.

Vare, J. W., & Miller, K. S. (2000). Integrating caring across the curriculum. *ERS Spectrum, 18*(1), 27–35.

Wagner, T. (1999, May 12). Reflections on Columbine: Standards for the heart? *Education Week*, 48, 33.

Warren, M., Hong, S. L., Rubin, C., & Uy, P. S. (2009). Beyond the bake sale: A community-based relational approach to parent engagement in schools. *Teachers College Record, 111*(9), 2209–2254.

Wessler, S. L. (2001). Sticks and stones. *Educational Leadership, 58*(4), 28–33.

White, R., Algozzine, B., Audette, R., Marr, M. B., & Ellis, E. D., Jr. (2001). Unified discipline: A school-wide approach for managing problem behavior. *Intervention in School and Clinic, 37*(1), 3–8.

Willard, N. (2006, April 5). Cyberbullying: What educators need to know to combat online cruelty. *Education Week, 25*(30), 41, 43. Accessed at www.edweek.org/ew/articles/2010/06/30/36willard.h29.html?print=1 on April 27, 2012.

Wilson, B. L., & Corbett, H. D. (2001). *Listening to urban kids: School reform and the teachers they want*. Albany: State University of New York Press.

Youngerman, S. (1998). The power of cross-level partnerships. *Educational Leadership, 56*(1), 58–60.

INDEX

Data-Based Decision Making, Third Edition
Edie L. Holcomb

You're ready to start collecting school data, but what data? How will you find it, and how will you use it once you have it? An informative resource for elementary school principals, this book takes an in-depth look at best data collection practice for schoolwide improvement.

BKF469

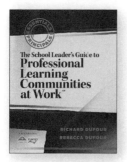

The School Leader's Guide to Professional Learning Communities at Work™
Richard DuFour and Rebecca DuFour

Are you a K–8 principal looking to implement the PLC at Work™ process? Explore the components needed to lay the foundation, including how to develop a structure that supports collaborative teams, how to focus on effective monitoring strategies, and more.

BKF489

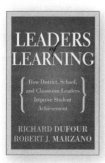

Leaders of Learning
Richard DuFour and Robert J. Marzano

Together, the authors focus on district leadership, principal leadership, and team leadership and address how individual teachers can be most effective in leading students—by learning with colleagues how to implement the most promising pedagogy in their classrooms.

BKF455

The Will to Lead, the Skill to Teach
Anthony Muhammad and Sharroky Hollie

The authors acknowledge both the structural and sociological issues that contribute to low-performing schools and offer multiple tools and strategies to assess and improve classroom management, increase literacy, establish academic vocabulary, and contribute to a healthier school culture.

BKF443

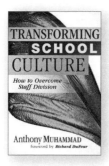

Transforming School Culture
Anthony Muhammad

Busy administrators will appreciate this quick read packed with immediate, accessible strategies. This book provides the framework for understanding dynamic relationships within a school culture and ensuring a positive environment that supports the changes necessary to improve learning for all students.

BKF281

Solution Tree | Press *a division of* Solution Tree

Visit solution-tree.com or call 800.733.6786 to order.

Solution Tree

Solution Tree's mission is to advance the work of our authors. By working with the best researchers and educators worldwide, we strive to be the premier provider of innovative publishing, in-demand events, and inspired professional development designed to transform education to ensure that all students learn.

The mission of the National Association of Elementary School Principals is to lead in the advocacy and support for elementary and middle level principals and other education leaders in their commitment for all children.